Mancheste

Manchester Architecture Guide is the first in the new Manchester Guides series. It is designed as a practical street guide to Manchester city centre's significant buildings. Descriptions of 69 buildings are organised into 6 walks which refer to a map and which cater for your need for refreshment. A potted history of Manchester's architectural history is supported by useful indexes of architects and buildings as well as a glossary. We thoroughly recommend looking out for buildings not selected for this guide: you will be richly rewarded for your curiosity.

Contents:

Introduction 2 – 3
Map 4 – 5
Chronological Index 6

Route 1
Manchester Cathedral to Trinity Bridge 9 – 27

Route 2
Crown Square to Manchester Town Hall 31 – 55

Route 3
Liverpool Road Station to the Midland Hotel 59 – 73

Route 4
City Art Gallery to Portico Library 77 – 97

Route 5
Manchester Evening News Arena to Rochdale Canal 101 – 115

Route 6
Oxford Road Train Station to Quay Bar 119 – 143

Index of Architects 144 – 145
Glossary 146 – 148

Introduction

Manchester's Development: An outline

This is a timely moment to produce a new architectural guide to Manchester. The city is experiencing a periodic upheaval of redevelopment, and all who have a regard for it should take stock of the process.

At first sight Manchester is not an easy city to read. Some regard it as deficient because it lacks the geometric formalities of squares and vistas, but it has a legible structure that derives from its historic, organic growth, and it has a grain and its own subtleties. For geographic reasons it spread south and east from its medieval site *(see the Cathedral and Chethams pages 9 & 11)* and the Georgian 'new town' was centred on St Ann's Square and its fine church *(page 21)*. After 1764, when the canal system and, later, industrialisation arrived, they skirted the town, which remained residential. Only fragments survive of Georgian Manchester but these include the Royal Manchester Institution, 1824-35, now the City Art Gallery *(page 77)* and one or two other small public buildings. It was commerce not industry that cleared the Georgian streets and created the Victorian city that largely survives today. The commercial incursion began on the north side of Market Street, as is still evident, and spread to its south in the 1830s. By the 1870s it was all but complete.

As the centre of a great industrial region and the focal point of a world market, the city enjoyed both wealth and political influence. It expressed its status through its architecture. In its prime its buildings were leading examples of their time and they remain architecturally significant today. Examples which figure in this guide are Cockerell's Bank of England *(page 35)*, the Free Trade Hall *(page 67)* and that great classic, Waterhouse's Town Hall *(page 55)*. Manchester's heritage, however, cannot be confined to a handful of famous buildings. Apart from the grand examples there are numerous other buildings of interest or distinction, and the surviving Victorian streets provide an urban context that is humane, strongly consistent in scale, rich and inventive in detail and character, and harmonious through the use of a range of attractive and suitable materials. At its best Manchester's environment satisfies the mind, stirs the imagination and pleases the eye. Properly understood it is a valuable asset to the city, and residents long familiar with its streets are sometimes surprised to find that visitors, whether native or foreign, are often quick to appreciate the qualities that give it identity. It is highly appropriate that most of the city centre is covered by conservation areas.

Part of the city's heritage is an intricate network of footpaths, passages and minor roads that make it convenient to walk across the city. The pedestrianisation of streets and squares such as Brazennose Street, King Street and St Ann's Square has also been beneficial and heightens the appreciation of architectural and urban qualities.

During the first half of the 20th century the city centre remained almost static, although the civic area was extended by the creation of St Peter's Square and the building of the Central Library and the Town Hall Extension *(pages 45 & 47)*. After World War II redevelopment became inevitable. Principally it was related to the replacement of war-damaged or run-down areas, and the major examples are Crown Square *(page 31)*, Piccadilly Plaza *(page 93)* and the Arndale Centre *(page 17)*. The city's changed circumstances are revealed by the architecture. Manchester was no longer at the leading edge in patronage and design and much of the contemporary building is mediocre. However even this has its lessons, and from the rebuilding of Portland Street it can be seen how a misapplied concept of modernism, in this case the introduction of high-rise towers, has proved totally disruptive to a street which should have been the architectural spine of the area. Positive lessons can be found elsewhere in the excellence of the CIS offices on Miller Street *(page 105)*, where the high towers are on the edge of the city, and in other buildings such as 55 King Street, commissioned by the District Bank *(page 37)*, and its neighbour Pall Mall Court. Manchester also can show some exemplary and imaginative adaptations of historic buildings to modern use. Foremost is the Royal Exchange Theatre *(page 19)* and another is the conversion of a railway warehouse into the Museum of Science and Industry. Other commendable but more straightforward illustrations of conservation are to be found at the same museum *(page 59)*, the Daily Express Building *(page 107)*, and, on a smaller scale, the Merchants' Warehouse, Castlefield, a model of its kind.

Largely on the evidence shown in the last section of the Guide, some Manchester architects claim that the city is now experiencing a renaissance but, despite promising signs, it is too early to ascertain this. There are some stylish small buildings and coffee bars, but the one large building, the Bridgewater Hall *(page 133)*, although impressive internally appears unrelated to its neighbours and the city. Also the paved area in front of it, named Barbirolli Square, represents the misapplication of a prestigious name to a space that provides neither enclosure nor protection from the elements. Other recent developments have included the generally successful conversion of the Castlefield canal basin to leisure use. Currently several major schemes are in progress and others are proposed. They can be regarded as test cases of the balance between commercialism and informed planning and design that respects the growth and grain of the city, not to mention its climate. This guide, with its colourful images, should encourage appreciation of the city's architecture and heritage; it is hoped also that it will lead to a much wider interest in and discussion of the city's planning and its future.

John H.G. Archer

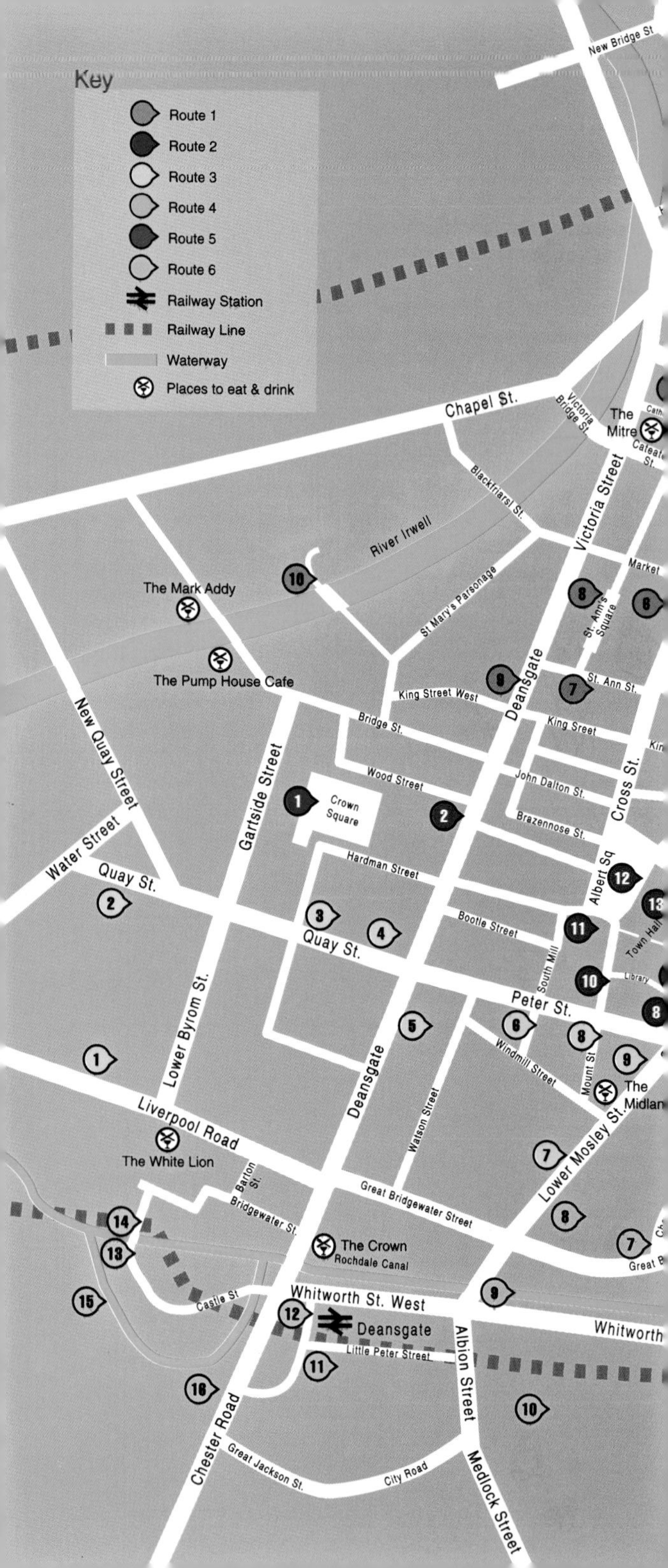
Key
Route 1
Route 2
Route 3
Route 4
Route 5
Route 6
Railway Station
Railway Line
Waterway
Places to eat & drink
New Bridge St
Chapel St.
Victoria Bridge St.
The Mitre
Cateaton St.
Blackfriars St.
Victoria Street
River Irwell
Market
The Mark Addy
St Mary's Parsonage
St. Ann's Square
The Pump House Cafe
Deansgate
St. Ann St.
King Street West
Bridge St.
King Sreet
Gartside Street
New Quay Street
Wood Street
John Dalton St.
Crown Square
Cross St.
Brazennose St.
Water Street
Hardman Street
Albert Sq
Quay St.
Bootle Street
Town Hall
Quay St.
South Mill
Library
Peter St.
Lower Byrom St.
Windmill Street
Mount St
The Midlan
Liverpool Road
Watson Street
Lower Mosley St.
The White Lion
Barton St.
Great Bridgewater Street
Bridgewater St.
The Crown
Rochdale Canal
Great B
Castle St
Whitworth St. West
Whitworth
Deansgate
Little Peter Street
Albion Street
Chester Road
Great Jackson St.
City Road
Medlock Street

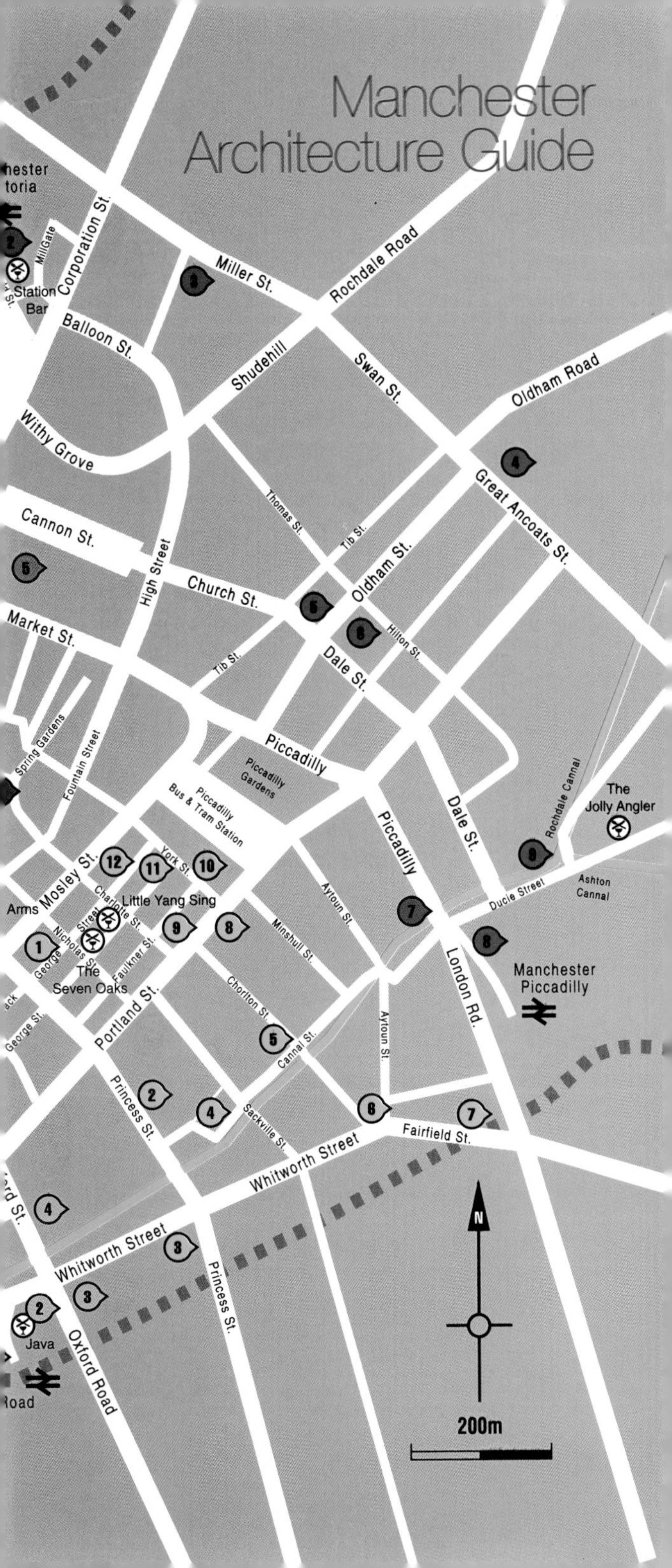
Manchester
Architecture Guide
Corporation St.
Miller St.
Rochdale Road
Station Bar
Balloon St.
Shudehill
Swan St.
Oldham Road
Withy Grove
Thomas St.
Tib St.
Great Ancoats St.
Cannon St.
High Street
Church St.
Oldham St.
Hilton St.
Market St.
Tib St.
Dale St.
Spring Gardens
Fountain Street
Piccadilly
Piccadilly Gardens
Piccadilly Bus & Tram Station
Piccadilly
Dale St.
Rochdale Canal
The Jolly Angler
Mosley St.
York St.
Little Yang Sing
Charlotte St.
Aytoun St.
Ducie Street
Ashton Canal
Arms
George Street
Nicholas St.
The Seven Oaks
Faulkner St.
Minshull St.
London Rd.
Manchester Piccadilly
Chorlton St.
George St.
Portland St.
Aytoun St.
Canal St.
Princess St.
Sackville St.
Fairfield St.
Whitworth Street
Whitworth Street
Princess St.
Java
Oxford Road
N
200m

Chronological Index (completion dates)

1421 **Manchester Cathedral** 9
1422 **Chetham's School** 11
1600s **Sinclair's Oyster Bar & the Old Wellington Inn** 15
1712 **St. Ann's Church** 21
1805 **Rochdale Canal** 115
1806 **Portico Library/The Bank** 97
c.1820 **Peveril of the Peak** 131
1828 **Friends' Meeting House** 49
1830 **Liverpool Road Station and Museum of Science & Industry** 59
1835 **City Art Gallery** 77
1844 **Victoria Station** 103
1846 **Former Bank of England** 35
1851 **S. & J. Watts Warehouse/ Britannia Hotel** 89
1854 **National Museum of Labour History/ Mechanics' Institute** 79
1856 **Free Trade Hall** 67
1862 **Albert Memorial** 53
1865 **Memorial Hall/ Square Albert** 51
1871 **Barton Arcade** 23
1877 **Manchester Town Hall** 55
1879 **Central Station/GMEX** 69
c.1880 **Castlefield Viaduct** 139
1885 **Manchester Law Library** 41
1891 **Refuge Assurance/ Palace Hotel** 123
1896 **Great Northern Railway Co. Goods Warehouse** 65
1899 **Rylands Library** 33
1903 **Corn Exchange** 13
1903 **Midland Hotel** 73
1905 **Joshua Hoyle &Co./ Malmaison Hotel** 111
1906 **London Road Fire Station** 87
1909 **Canada House** 127
1909 **Y.M.C.A./ St. George's House** 71
1912 **Opera House** 63
1912 **St. James' Buildings** 125
1912 **Lancaster House** 81
1921 **Royal Exchange & Royal Exchange Theatre** 19
1924 **Cenotaph** 43
1929 **Midland Bank** 39
1931 **Lee House** 129
1932 **Sunlight House** 65
1934 **Central Reference Library** 65
1938 **Town Hall Extension**
1939 **Daily Express** 47
1939 **Kendal's** 25
1960 **Oxford Road Train Station** 119
1962 **Crown Court** Crown Square 31
1962 **CIS Tower** 105
1962 **Granada Television** 61
1965 **Scottish Life House** (now Manchester House) Crown Square 31
1965 **Piccadilly Plaza** 73
1967 **Telephone Exchange/ Rutherford House** 95
1967 **Cumberland House** Crown Square 31
1969 **Former Nat West Bank Northern Headquarters** 37
1969 **Gateway House** 113
1971 **Magistrates' Court** Crown Square 31
1971 **Bank of England** 91
1979 **Arndale Centre** 17
1982 **The Hacienda:Fac 51** 135
1985 **Cornerhouse Arts Centre** 121
1989 **Manto** 83
1989 **Dry 201** 109
1991 **British Council HQ/ British Telecom** 135
1994 **Atlas** 137
1994 **Manchester Metropolitan University Aytoun Library** 85
1995 **Nynex Arena/Manchester Evening News Arena** 101
1995 **Planet 4 Studios** 137
1996 **Trinity Bridge** 27
1996 **Bridgewater Hall** 133
1996 **Merchants Bridge** 141
1996 **Mash & Air** 83
1996 **Barça** 139
1998 **Urban Splash/ Smithfield Buildings** 109
1998 **Quay Bar** 143

Route 1

Recommended Places
To Eat & Drink

Mitre Hotel *Cathedral Yard*
Mark Addy *New Bailey Street*

1. Manchester Cathedral Grade I

Fennel Street

Original architects unknown (1421)

Alterations and restorations:

J.P. Holden (1815 and 1868)

J.S. Crowther (1886)

Basil Champneys (1898 and 1903)

Sir Percy Worthington (1934)

Sir Hubert Worthington (post-1940)

The Cathedral Church of St. Mary, St. Denys and St. George was originally a collegiate church founded by the Lord of the Manor Thomas de la Warre in 1421. Raised to cathedral status in 1847, its position in the medieval core of Manchester has left it isolated on the edge of the city's commercial centre. The original late Gothic structure has been surrounded and engulfed by 19th century and later additions. Although the most significant surviving medieval building in the city, the external appearance is largely the result of these additions, especially the raising of the tower in 1867 and the creation of the new west porch in 1898. Internally, the elaborate timber choir stalls are remarkable, especially for the humour of the miséricord carving (which include pigs dancing and playing the bagpipes, a rabbit cooking the hunter, and a man apparently breaking his wife's cooking pot). Following the I.R.A. bomb of 1996 a new urban plan for Manchester (currently under construction) attempts to integrate this important historic fragment into the contemporary centre by the building of New Cathedral Street.

2. Chetham's School Grade I

Long Millgate

Original architects unknown (1422)

Restorations and additions:

Alfred Waterhouse (1878)

Oliver & Charles Heywood (1885)

Established as domestic accommodation for his collegiate church by Thomas de la Warre, the core of this complex has survived the Dissolution of the Monasteries and sequestration under Cromwell. The executors of the local philanthropist Humphrey Chetham purchased the buildings for use as a charity school and library in 1654, and it retains its educational function to this day, specialising in music. The buildings present an open-sided courtyard to the northern flank of the cathedral, its two storey ranges having late Gothic arches and a patterning of small double and triple bayed tracery windows beneath a large roof. The rear elevation is of particular architectural merit, with its dramatic chimneys and projecting bays, the result of a seamless upgrading in 1902. None of the other buildings, such as those by Alfred Waterhouse for the Manchester Grammar School, have any of the integrity of the original buildings. Internally, there remains a Great Hall and a panelled reading room, the home of Chetham's library.

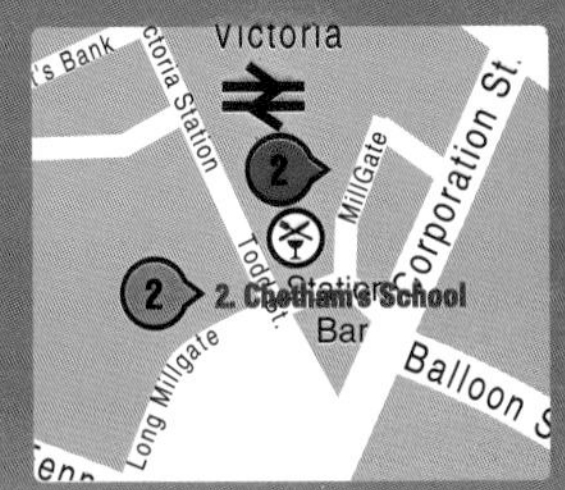

TRIANGLE

3. Corn Exchange Grade II

Hanging Ditch

Potts, Son & Pickup (1903)

Originally a produce exchange and then a flea market, the Corn Exchange occupies a medieval triangular block adjacent to the cathedral and presents eclectic Renaissance façades (stylistically conservative for its time) in each direction. Acute corners provide opportunities to exaggerate the vertical emphasis of much of these broad surfaces. The entrance lobbies display combinations of marble, tiling and carved timber, while the centre is occupied by a broad glazed dome. Having suffered severe structural damage from the I.R.A. bomb, the refurbished building will be adapted to more contemporary commercial needs as the northern focus of New Cathedral Street.

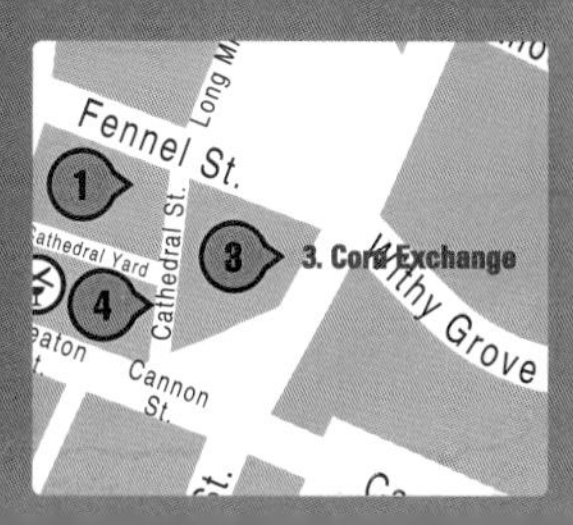

Samuel Smith
SINCLAIRS

4. Sinclair's Oyster Bar & the Old Wellington Inn Grade II

Cathedral Yard

Original architects unknown

(reconstruction 1999)

C.17th century and primarily timber-framed structures, these two buildings are undergoing their second reincarnation in 30 years. Originally sited on Manchester's market place, they were raised by an indeterminate amount above their original street level to form a townscape feature in the centre of the 1960s commercial development of Shambles Square. The inherent flexibility of their structure allowed them to survive the impact of the I.R.A. bomb largely unscathed. However they lay in the path of the proposed Exchange Street, and have therefore been carefully taken apart and re-erected over one hundred metres to the north. Here they will sit next to the cathedral and the refurbished Corn Exchange, a relocated historical fragment reinforcing the "heritage" value of this quarter. Because of their peripatetic history, much of what is visible to the eye is a simulation of traditional construction.

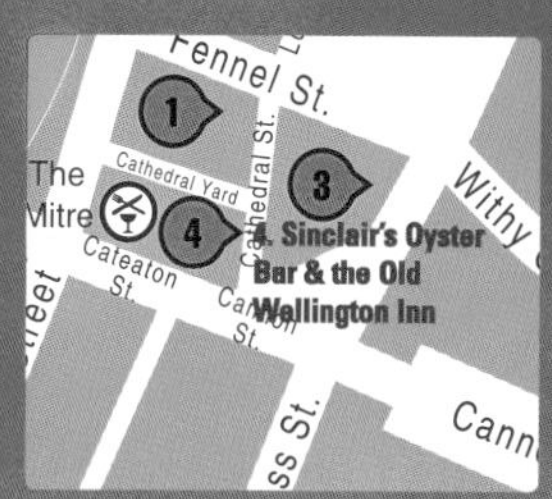

Bhs
Bhs
JJB
JJB SPORTS
STOP

5. Arndale Centre

Market Street

Wilson & Wormersley (1979)

Obliterating 8 city blocks, the Arndale Centre is an built example of the brave new world of retail c. 1965. This huge structure accommodates retail, a covered market, multi-storey car parking, bus garage, roof top housing and offices. Its buff-coloured tiled bulk stretches the full length of Market Street, engulfs Cannon Street and meets Cross Street and Shudehill as an impenetrable wall with cavernous service entrances. The High Street elevation is characterised by extensive horizontal car parking decks and a brown spiral car ramp.

Internally, a recent refurbishment tried to humanise this giant shopping machine which remains the epitome of privately owned public space. Glazed atria and an assortment of late post-modern design features attempt to give identifiable character to the arcades. The Arndale Centre currently holds one of Manchester's most unusual spaces, Barbirolli Square, home to a giant Foghorn Leghorn. The Cross Street elevation was extensively damaged in the 1996 I.R.A. bomb which briefly threatened the building's future. Its entire length, at the time of writing clad in silver corrugated sheeting, is to be remodelled to meet the needs of shoppers in the new millennium, linked to the rebuilt Marks & Spencer by a new bridge designed by Manchester architects Hodder Associates.

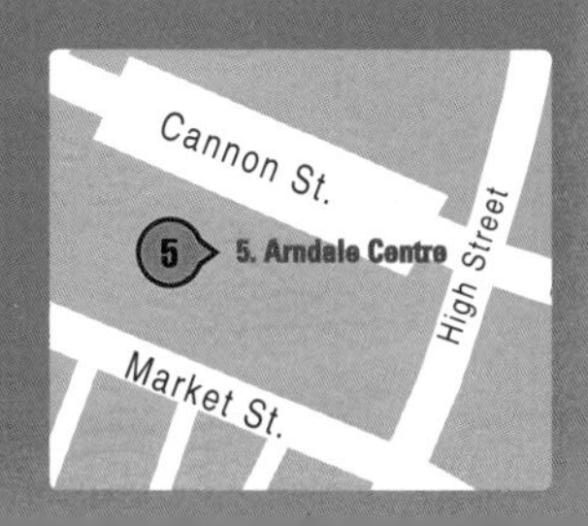

6. Royal Exchange & Royal Exchange Theatre Grade II

St. Ann's Square / Exchange Street and Cross Street

Bradshaw, Gass & Hope (1921)

Levitt Bernstein (1976; 1998)

Structurally damaged in the I.R.A. bomb, the Royal Exchange is the former home of the cotton trade in Manchester. It was built on the original marketplace and its present exterior masks the piecemeal story of its growth. A substantial stone base is topped by a gigantic engaged Corinthian order with an attic above. One of the two glass roofs was destroyed during World War 2, while reduced trade continued beneath the other until the mid-1960s. 10 years later the lunar module-inspired theatre was introduced and a successful new life for the building was achieved. Within the ornate classical interior, the Hi Tech auditorium is supported off the concealed steel structure and integrates very well despite the radical differences in style. The post-bomb refurbishment has introduced a vivid colour scheme.

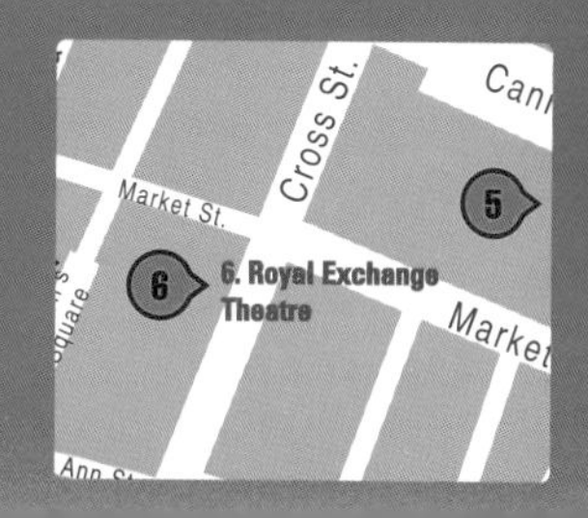

7. St. Ann's Church Grade I

St Ann's Square

Sir Christopher Wren or pupil (1712 onwards)

Restoration:

Alfred Waterhouse (1891)

Sometimes ascribed to Sir Christopher Wren or one of his pupils, St. Ann's has twofold significance: as part of an urban ensemble with St. Ann's Square, and as Manchester's oldest surviving Classical building. As such its distinguishing features include the round arched windows, the applied two-storey Corinthian pilasters, the semi-circular apse with giant order and the columned and pedimented doorways. Its galleried interior conforms to the pattern of churches of the period, although most of the furnishings are 19th century, including the stained glass salvaged following I.R.A. bomb damage in 1996. Prior to this attack however the dignity of the church and its square had already been compromised by the introduction of new landscape features (rewarded by the Civic Trust). Originally crowned by a tiered timber spire above the tower, much of the charm of the church itself derives from the patched quality of the sandstone and the sharpness of its details.

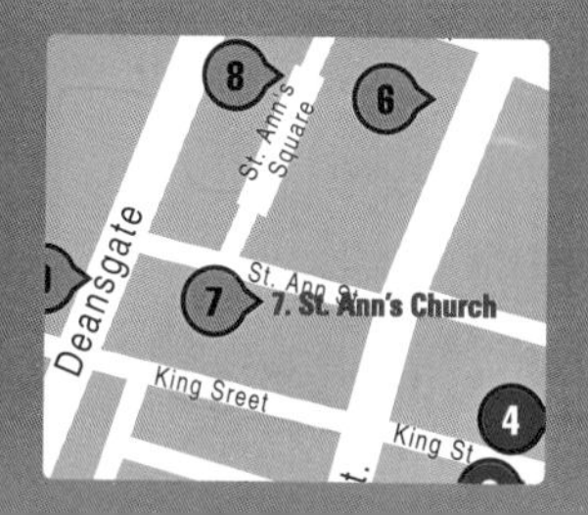

ARCADE

8. Barton Arcade Grade II*

51-63 Deansgate and Barton Square

Corbett, Raby & Sawyer (1871)

The epitome of commercial architecture in 19th Century Manchester, the façade to Deansgate fails to indicate the quality of the technologically advanced construction behind. Based around twin domes, the cast iron and glass roof covers a set of galleried spaces which house offices above ground level shops. Although the detail is delicate and traditional, the clear construction of the glass roof has a more organic character. Glimpses of the domes from St. Ann's Square and Ridgefield set a high standard for urban and architectural design which few subsequent commercial spaces in the city have emulated.

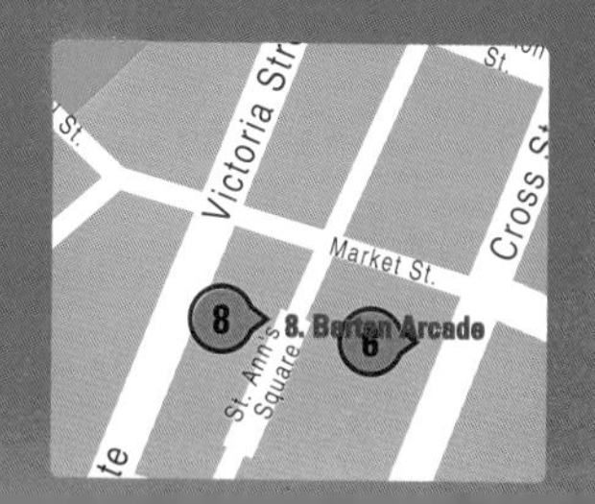

KENDALS

9. **Kendal's** (formerly Kendal Milne & Co. Ltd.) **Grade II**

98-116 Deansgate

J.S. Beaumont (1939)

Modelled on German department stores of the early 1930s by architects such as Erich Mendelsohn, Kendal's utilises modern materials such as glass block and Portland stone cladding to produce a clean and simple modernist exterior. This contrasts with the neo-classical style of its contemporaries in Manchester such as Lewis's on Piccadilly. Internally, the store has been extensively refitted so that customers are unaware of the innovative use of materials on the façade. Two banks of lifts sit beside escalators to the rear of the store. The entrances off Deansgate are characterised by their aroma, coffee in the delicatessen, perfume in the main store. These contrast with the labyrinthine 5th floor entrances via the multi-storey car park to the rear, where wealthy customers have their cars valeted while they shop.

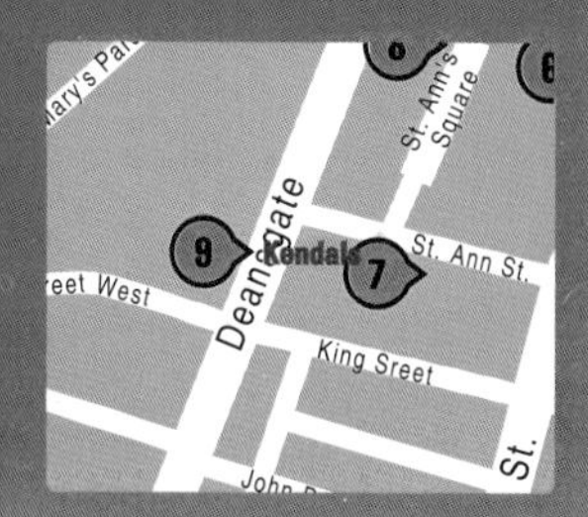

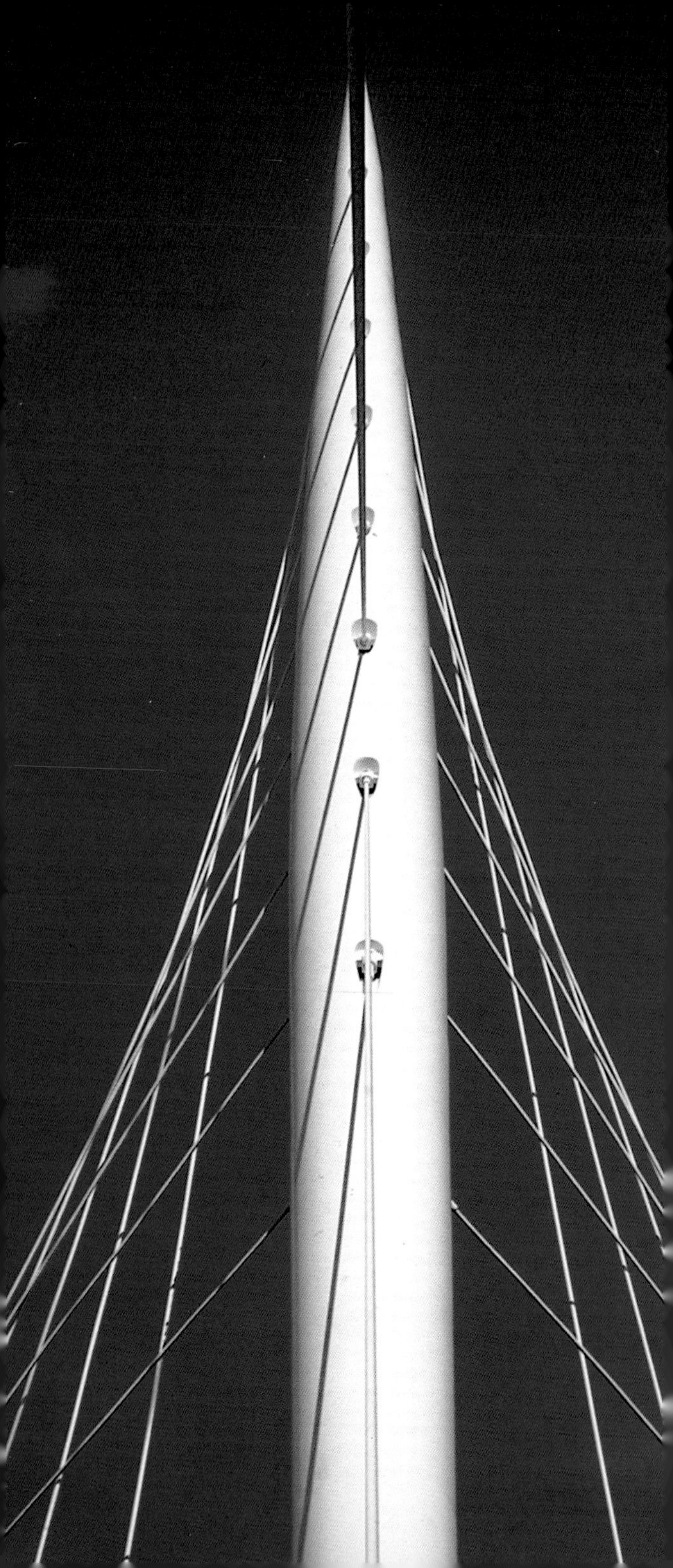

10. Trinity Bridge

St. Mary's Parsonage

Santiago Calatrava (1996)

The cities of Manchester and Salford, traditional rivals divided by the River Irwell, agreed this bridge as an opportunity to present a new partnership through the design of a flagship footbridge. Spanish engineer Calatrava produced an elegant tour de force. A single raking strut on the Salford side supports the Y-shaped bridge and ramp by tension cables. Sculpturally elegant, the bridge represents an aspiration for the development of the area as a business district. Its alien form is enhanced by a curiously arbitrary landscape design at the riversides, bearing no relation to the bridge or the wider context.

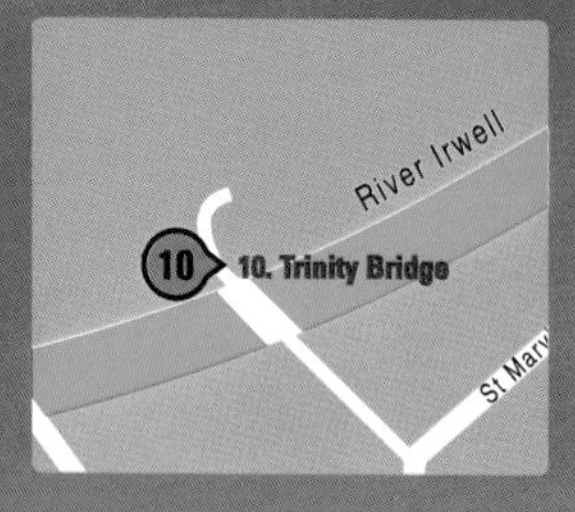

Route

2

Recommended Places To Eat & Drink

Pump House Cafe *Bridge Street*
City Arms *Kennedy Street*

1. Crown Square

Manchester City Architect L.C. Howitt (1962)
Magistrates' Court: Yorke, Rosenberg & Mardall (1971)
Cumberland House: Leach, Rhodes & Walker (1967)
Scottish Life House (now Manchester House): Leach Rhodes & Walker (1965)

Crown Square and its surrounding buildings are the result of the radical 1945 City of Manchester Plan for the creation of an extended civic axis based on the Town Hall clock tower (although the tower itself was to have been replaced). The square is bordered by civic and judicial buildings, all constructed within a decade of each other. The earliest building in this grouping is the Portland stone clad Crown Court, a stripped Modern interpretation of Classicism. Its uninspiring composition features a raised central entrance with a particularly effete eagle-bedecked canopy, with the courts behind visible through double height glazing. The Magistrate's Court by YRM sits on a raised plinth and generous forecourt above layers of parking, a service yard and a cafeteria. The Modernist tiled white frame encloses a dark glass box in a minimalist cubic composition that reflects the spatial organisation within. The courts are in the middle of the building, surrounded by double height spaces and single storey administrative offices. The blind top storey houses the cells and servicing plant. The building authoritatively closes the space on the southern side of Crown Square. The east side of the square is defined by Cumberland House, home of several local authority departments. A polite composition of dark brick and steel framed bays over a white stone plinth, the building edges an empty public space between Crown Square and Spinningfield. On the north side is Manchester House, a white 8 storey square tower of offices on a two storey podium in a commercial Modernist style, and the Crown Court extension. This Late Modern composition of splayed windows in Portland stone is redolent of the dying days of the Property Services Agency as an arm of government.

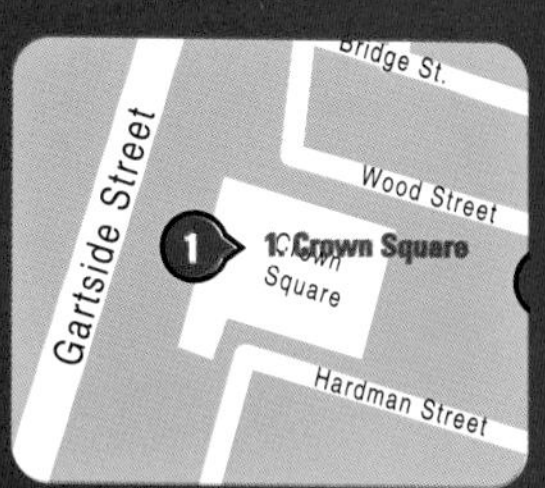

2. Rylands Library Grade I

Deansgate

Basil Champneys (1899)

Now owned by the University of Manchester, the library was built by Enriqueta Augustina Rylands as a memorial to her husband, the local textile manufacturer John Rylands. The last significant flowering of Gothic in the city, the library reworks a religious theme with a soaring nave to impress visitors and intimate panelled reading alcoves occupying the aisles. This space is reached from a generous stair hall featuring compressed ranks of slender columns and tantalising views through distant lanterns. Constructed of a deep red sandstone, the quality of metalwork and joinery is superb. The nostalgia of the detail conceals the fact of the library's technological sophistication, with heating and ventilation fully integrated into the design, and readers assisted by early electric work lights and chandeliers. However, the character of the building is generally monastic, reflecting the theological basis of Rylands's own collection of books and manuscripts around which the library was formed.

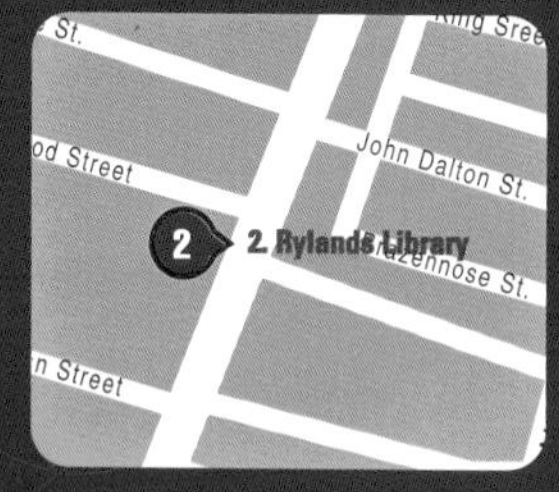

3. Former Bank of England

Grade I

82 King Street

Charles Robert Cockerell (1846)

Tower addition:

Holford Associates (1995)

Built as a branch office of the Bank of England, this fine building demonstrates both the archaeological skill and architectural inventiveness of Cockerell. A major figure of 19th century British architecture, his work is commemorated by a blue plaque on the façade. The austere side elevations adjoin a complex frontispiece to King Street which freely combines Greek and Roman precedents. Engaged Doric columns support an attic and pediment containing a small Serlian motif. These elements frame three thermal windows and a doorway (a late 19th century insertion) which light the former banking hall with its central barrel vault. However, the original entrance was the arched opening on to Pall Mall, reinstated during the building's conversion by Holford Associates into a lobby for their new post-modern office tower behind, which attempts a sympathetic relationship to this exquisite building.

4. Former National Westminster Bank Northern Headquarters

55 King Street

Casson Conder & Partners (1969)

This building demonstrates a skilled and inventive architectural interpretation of the shift away from International Style modernism. The sheer black ribbed granite façade employs a language of highly abstracted traditional forms. Fortress-like, it terminates in a quasi-mansard roof although the flush-set glazing is far from traditional. The gaunt verticality of the exterior contrasts with the smooth white marble-lined horizontality of the banking hall. Externally, the building defines one edge of a sheltered plaza over a parking deck. The changing character of this end of King Street is expected to result in the building's conversion to retail use in the near future.

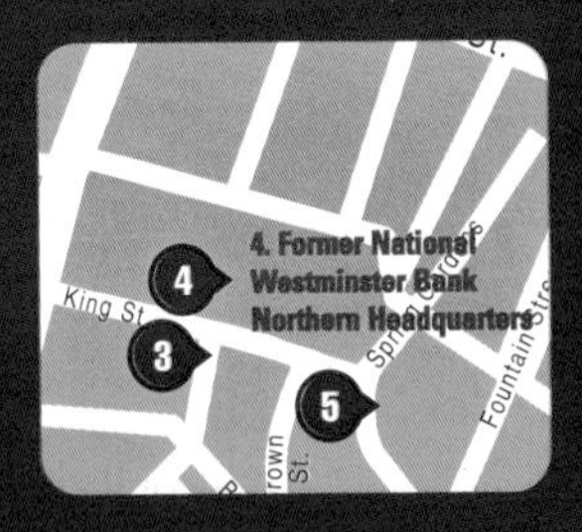

Midland Bank
Midland Bank

5. Midland Bank Grade II*

100 King Street

Sir Edwin Lutyens with Whinney, Son & Ansten Hall (1929)

One of a number of banks produced for this client in the 1920s, here Lutyens plays with a ziggurat motif in the mathematical setbacks he also employed for the Thiepval Arch and the unfinished Metropolitan Cathedral in Liverpool. Sheer ashlar walling separates classical motifs at the apex and base where he employs a characteristic device of a pilaster disappearing into rustication. The exterior form is geometrically composed with a large amount of unadorned wall space. Internally, the banking hall uses the Delhi Order with its suspended bells which the architect had invented for the contemporary Viceroy of India's House.

NCHESTER
LIBRARY

6. Manchester Law Library

Grade II*

14, Kennedy Street

Thomas Hartas (1885)

A sensitive and delicate infill building for the dense and thriving city, the Law Library is an essay in mid-19th century Venetian Gothic, and is the most elaborate façade in a series of interesting examples along Kennedy Street. Three storeys are divided into three bays which themselves have three divisions. This playfulness continues with the deep carving of the window surrounds and tracery elements, and these recessions promote the dematerialisation of the façade with its pierced entrance screen in the lower right-hand corner and centrally placed projecting oriel window.

7. Cenotaph Grade II*

St. Peter's Square

Sir Edwin Lutyens (1924)

Similar to his design in Whitehall, London, the Cenotaph forms a sombre composition with its backdrop of Central Library. Its white Portland stone form stands on the site of St. Peter's Church, demolished in 1907. Axially aligned with Mosley Street, the monument suffers in its current context from the clutter created by the new Metrolink tram stop. Although the seating is well used by office workers at lunch time and for annual remembrance parades, the central pylon and its subsidiary cross and obelisks have insufficient scale to read effectively against the varying quality of the buildings around the square. The gravitas of Lutyens's monument is particularly diminished by the poor examples of recent public art which have followed it.

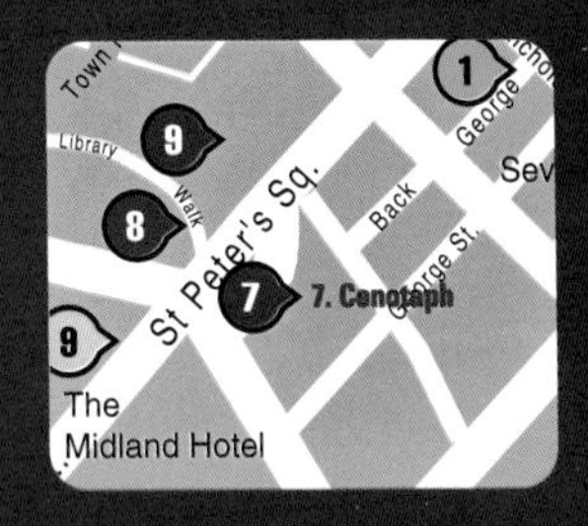

8. Central Reference Library

Grade II*

St. Peter's Square

E. Vincent Harris (1934)

Originally designed as a 1925 competition entry with the Town Hall Extension, Harris employed a cunning circular design to mask the misalignments of Oxford Street and Peter Street, creating as a by-product the dramatic sweeping space of Library Walk. Central Library forms a major pivot in the city's most prestigious civic quarter. Its huge drum-like external wall is treated in a restrained manner, topped by a line of Doric columns, while the massive scale of the Corinthian portico to St. Peter's Square acts as an urban focus from considerable distance. Internally, the domed principal reading room at first floor level, inspired by the Pantheon in Rome, affords an opulent if echoing place for study.

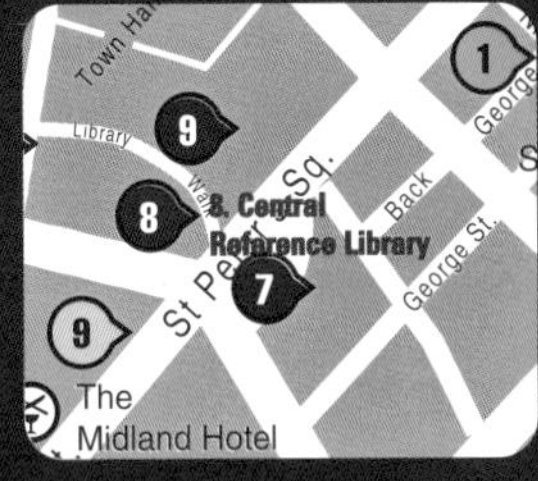

9. Town Hall Extension Grade II*

St. Peter's Square

E. Vincent Harris (1938)

Successfully resolving the difficult conundrum of style and space between Waterhouse's triangular Town Hall (see page 55) and Harris's earlier cylindrical Central Library (see page 45), the building defines two streets of contrasting character. Lloyd Street is a canyon animated by bridges linking the Town Hall and its extension. Library Walk is a dramatic unfolding space which frames Lutyens's Cenotaph (see page 43) in St. Peter's Square and the Ionic temple front of the Friends' Meeting House (see page 49) on Mount Street. The architectural clarity of the Rates Hall, internal counterpart to Library Walk, has been lost with the introduction of a bürolandschaft office plan attempting to 'humanise' a previously clearly hierarchical space.

FRIENDS MEETING HOUSE

10. Friends' Meeting House

Grade II

Mount Street

Richard Lane (1828)

Suggesting the importance of nonconformism in the developing industrial town, the scale of this block has subsequently been dwarfed by its neighbours. Still partly in use by the Quakers, the building has survived many attempts at redevelopment. Its front is raised up from street level on a podium with broad steps. These lead to an engaged Ionic portico in ashlar, with a much plainer brick building behind. It is a reticent but sturdy building befitting its congregation. Fortuitously, the classical frontispiece has been enhanced as a piece of townscape by the deference shown to it by E. Vincent Harris's design of Library Walk of a 100 years later.

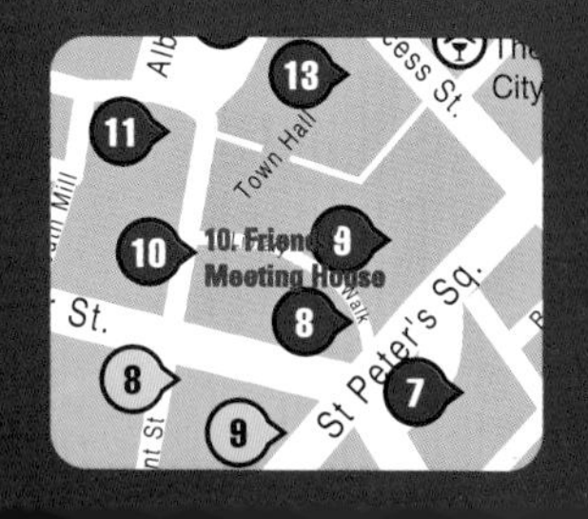

mma
Budweiser
HIT THE BAR!
WORLD CUP COVERAGE
SQUARE THE ALBERT

11. Memorial Hall/ Square Albert Grade II*

14 Albert Square

Thomas Worthington (1865)

Funded by the proceeds of the public collection for the Albert Memorial (see page 53), this building forms a corner of Albert Square. It memorialises a nonconformist secession of clerics of 1662, hence the use of that date on the façade. It exemplifies the influence of John Ruskin, especially his promotion of Venetian Gothic architecture as a model for 19th century mercantile cities. Polychrome brickwork, contrasting voussoirs, stone tracery and compositional asymmetry form a foil to a grander range of stone buildings on this side of the square. Its original users would probably be dismayed by its current use as a pub.

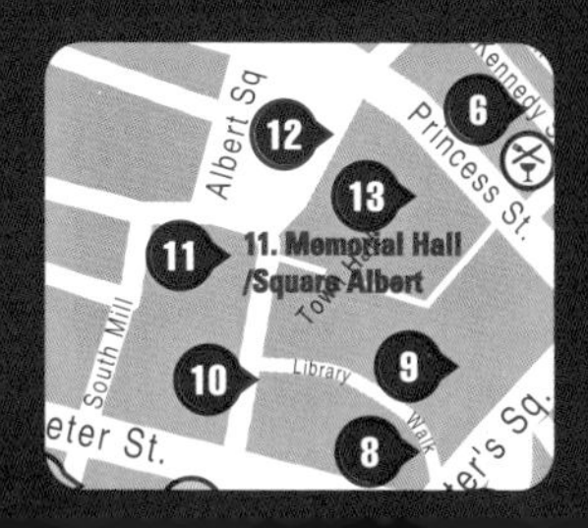

12. Albert Memorial Grade I

Albert Square

Thomas Worthington (1862)

Funded by public subscription during the national mourning for the Prince Consort and designed as a suitable receptacle to 'contain or cover' the statue (by Matthew Noble), Worthington chose a Gothic style to create an elaborate canopy topped by a spire. Elevated on a stepped plinth, the armorial decoration refers to Albert's Saxon origins, while his work in England is referred to by the small corner statues representing Art, Science, Agriculture and Commerce. These figures inhabit small corner tabernacles and were temporarily removed in the 1960s to reduce maintenance. Combining architectural and decorative motifs, this is the centrepiece of by far the best statuary group in the city and its setting was enhanced by the subsequent design of the Town Hall. (This statue predates the larger and more famous Albert Memorial in London by 15 months, and it is hard to believe that its design did not influence Sir George Gilbert Scott's work.)

13. Manchester Town Hall

Grade I

Albert Square

Alfred Waterhouse (1877)

Waterhouse cleverly adapted his French Gothic language to embody Mancunian civic pride on an awkward triangular site. The sandstone facing with its wealth of carving conceals a more utilitarian brick structure. A series of towers associated with the different entrances create a dramatic silhouette, while corner staircases conceal the differing floor heights between principal and subsidiary wings. The decorative themes continue into the low mosaiced entrance hall, where a shift in axial alignment passes almost unnoticed through the contrast between the stately ceremonial staircase and the minor spiral stair that speeds past it. The upper landing leads to the Great Hall with its murals of the history of Manchester by Ford Madox Brown.

Route 3

Recommended Places To Eat & Drink

White Lion *Liverpool Road*

Midland Hotel *Peter Street*

1. Liverpool Road Station and Museum of Science & Industry Grade I

Liverpool Road

George Stephenson for the Liverpool and Manchester Railway Company (1830)

The world's oldest passenger railway station, this building ceased passenger use in 1844 although it was still in use as a goods station as late as 1975. It is a late Georgian building and shows the difficulty engineers (and subsequently architects) had in adapting to the new age of steam. Incorporating an earlier house of 1808, the station is basically two storeys to accommodate access to the platform raised on an embankment behind. However, this commercial structure has elements of grandeur as befitted its use by passengers with first class tickets. Rustication on the lower storey is combined with an elemental applied portico with a three bayed window above. The rest of the building is smooth-faced with minimal mouldings, much of it reconstructed. Towards Deansgate the rendered elevation gives way to brickwork on the upper storey in acknowledgement of its less refined use for goods. The building is now both an exhibit of, and accommodation for, the Museum of Science and Industry (grade II listed).

GRANADA TELEVISIO

2. Granada Television

Quay Street

Ralph Tubbs (1962)

In contrast to the structural expressiveness of the architect's earlier Dome of Discovery at the Festival of Britain, this is a restrained work. A simple 8 storey slab block sits perpendicular to Quay Street, the language and materials reflecting the functional concerns of the architect. Blank gable walls are contrasted with glazed curtain walling to the main elevations. Lower level subsidiary buildings continue the architectural restraint of the main slab.

The muted quality of the buildings serves as a foil to the sculptural expressiveness of the cantilevered entrance canopy, heroic roof top spiral stair tower and the confident use of typography on entrance and roof top signage.

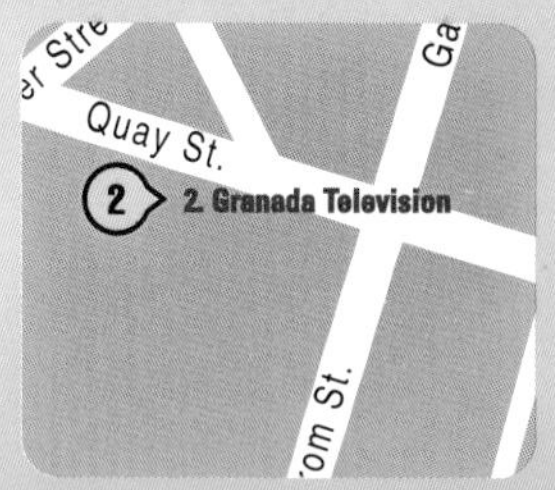

Oliver!
HOUSE
LADIES' NIGHT
OPERA HOUSE

3. Opera House Grade II

Quay Street

Richardson & Gill, with Farquarson (1912)

Designed as a new front to the pre-existing New Theatre, the exterior displays the imperial confidence of its date. Still in use as a theatre today, the Opera House is surmounted by a large pedimented gable. Stucco is used throughout the elaborate Classical language of the façade, unusual in having full height rustication. Giant order Ionic engaged fluted columns define a large central bay with the legend 'the play mirrors life' beneath a relief of Apollo on his chariot. Between the columns are inscribed the names of famous playwrights. The entrance canopy level is defined by a band of roses within a torus moulding. The pastel fancifulness towards Quay Street contrasts sharply with the simple red brick Byrom Street elevation.

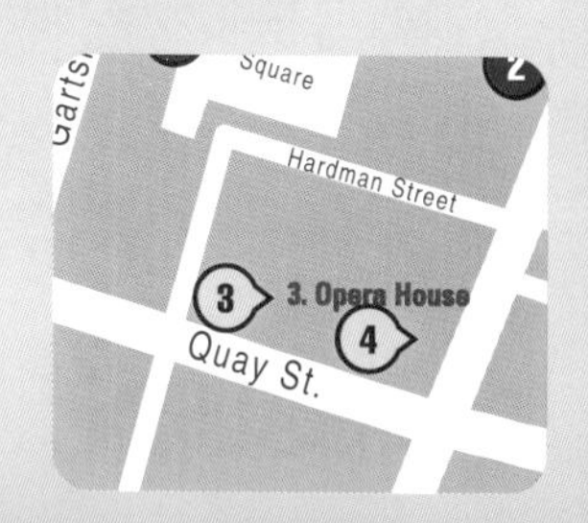

4. Sunlight House Grade II

85 Quay Street

Joseph Sunlight (1932)

The modern age is prefigured in this building, which was the first in Manchester to be taller than the Town Hall (see page 55). Its elements are stretched in an aspirational upward thrust from a muted classical base to an exaggerated mansard roof. Domed corner towers anchor the composition and provide access to layers of office accommodation above. Internally, the basement swimming pool beneath the lightwell is indicative of the glamorous lifestyle offered to the building's occupants and the aspirations of the architect. A convincing anecdote has it that Sunlight, an emigré, adopted his name from the popular soap brand of the same name on disembarking in Liverpool.

5. Great Northern Railway Company's Goods Warehouse

Grade II

Deansgate / Watson Street

Great Northern Railway Co. (1896)

Heroic in its form and elevated on a podium, this steel-framed warehouse is to be the centrepiece of a new commercial development. Largely hidden from Deansgate, the recent demolition of the corner with Peter Street has revealed the sublime bulk of the industrial structure behind the commercial street façade. Built at the level of the railway infrastructure in this part of the city, the warehouse has a monumental base of black engineering brick with four storeys of storage above in red brick with black brick and stone details. The building's name, picked out in white glazed brick, is the only ornament on this massive industrial beast.

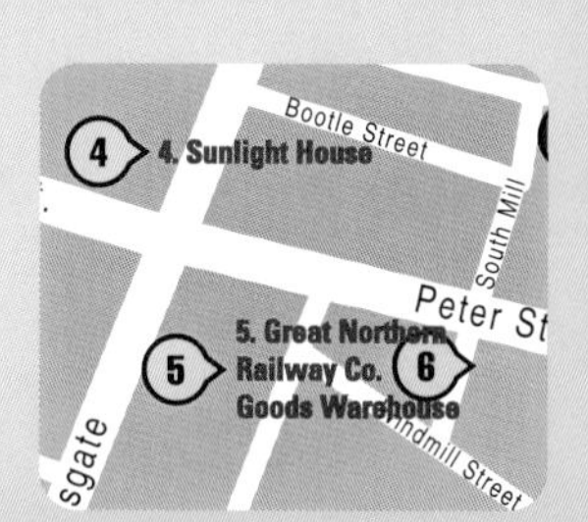

6. Free Trade Hall Grade II*

Peter Street

Edward Walters (1856)

L.C. Howitt, City Architect (1952)

Located on the site of the 1819 Peterloo Massacre, the Free Trade Hall commemorates the repeal of the Corn Law in 1846. The current building is the result of a marriage of two eras. The main façade to Peter Street is an elaborate and dignified essay in the Renaissance. Deeply modelled, its 9 bays are comprised of a square columned arcade slightly raised above street level, surmounted by *a piano nobile* of framed pedimented windows set within one and a half storey arches on coupled Ionic columns. Between the arches are roundels with a band of carved garlands topped by a deep cornice and balustrade. There are numerous references to the Free Trade and Anti-Corn Law Movement with allegorical carvings in the arcade and in the tympana of the first floor arches. The main façade continues for three bays into South Street where economy presides, the remainder being in a primitive Classical style.

The current interiors and the stark rear elevation are the result of rebuilding subsequent to WW2 bombing. The style could be described as Civic Neo-Scandinavian Classical. Notable are the 8 carved figures on the rear elevation representing activities in the Free Trade Hall's past. Following the Hallé Orchestra's move to the Bridgewater Hall (see page 133) the building remains empty. Its future is in question, but campaigners have recently thwarted an over-scaled hotel development which proposed using the existing façade to Peter Street as a podium for a 20 storey tower.

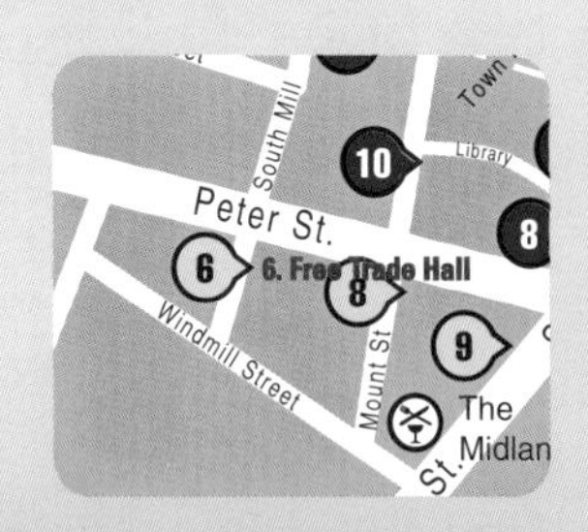

7. Central Station/GMEX Grade II*

Windmill Street

Sir John Fowler for the Midland Railway Co. (1879)
Essex Goodman & Suggit (1985)

Originally the railway terminus for transport from the west of the city centre, Central Station continued the role established by the Rochdale Canal and Castlefield Basin. Built over a complex layered urban fabric, a canal still runs beneath the building. The station shed, raised on its podium, is now approached by an extensive cobbled forecourt, where one would reasonably expect to find a hotel masking the shed. Following its closure in the 1960s its future remained uncertain until the shed was reconfigured into the exhibition and conference centre G-MEX. This provides an appropriate functional scale to use the whole of the station building effectively. However the banal smoked glass 'skirt' does not do justice to the quality of the heroic engineering structure it fronts.

SG
to let

8. Y.M.C.A./ St. George's House

Grade II

56-58 Peter Street

Woodhouse , Corbett & Dean (1909)

Austin Sztrala Turner (1992)

Important as an element in the sequence of Peter Street, this building survives now as an example of façade retention. This large terracotta block embodies the muscular Christianity of its original patrons, with taut horizontal bands of decoration controlling the dramatic asymmetries of the large entrance archway and shallow projecting bays. The roof structure (introduced when the building was gutted for office use) is unobtrusive from close views but protrudes to an unfortunate degree when seen from a distance. One is left nostalgic for the discretion with which the upper level swimming pool was treated by the original architects.

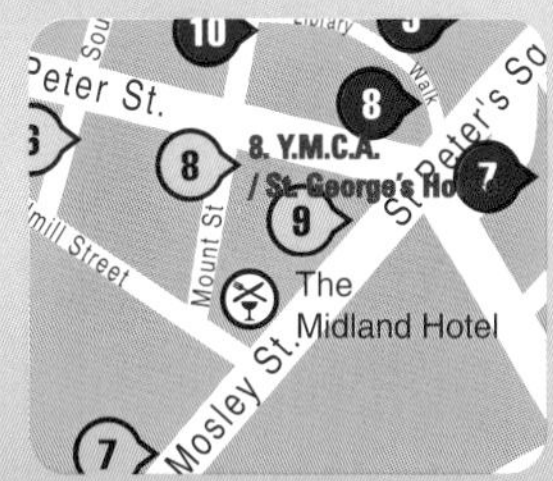

MIDLAND HOTEL
CROWNE
PLAZA

9. Midland Hotel Grade II*

Peter Street

Charles Trubshaw (1903)

A confection in reddish brown terracotta, red brick and polished granite, this elaborately decorated pile was built to provide hotel accommodation for the adjacent Central Station (see page 69) to which it was linked by a covered, glazed canopy. The exterior reflects the quality of the facilities within, which originally included a Winter Garden, Palm Court, Theatre, Concert Hall, and Continental restaurants. The architecture oozes unrestrained opulence to the detriment of its overall composition. This is a building as an assemblage of details, eclectically raiding and adapting styles as necessary. These include the muses overlooking Lower Mosley Street, an octagonal corner tower with lions rampant holding shields, a side entrance of volutes and heavily embellished Ionic column supporting a voluted roof, Neo-Dutch gables and Art Nouveau iron work.

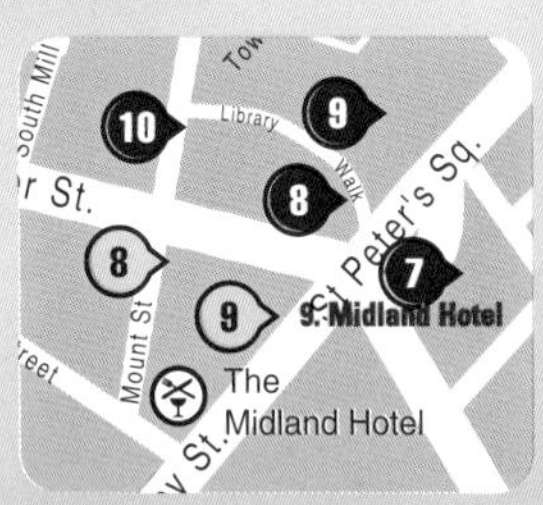

Route 4

Recommended Places To Eat & Drink

Seven Oaks *Nicholas Street*

Little Yang Sing *George Street*

1. City Art Gallery Grade I

Mosley Street

Sir Charles Barry (1835)

Constructed as the Royal Manchester Institution, Barry's only Greek Revival building integrates a graceful Ionic portico with a robust urban block. The delicacy of this arrangement continues internally with the immense height of the top-lit vestibule contrasting with its miniature Doric colonnade. The galleries were redecorated in High Victorian style in the 1890s to enhance the significant collection of paintings from this period. An extension designed by Sir Michael Hopkins and Partners is to be built to join the gallery to Barry's neighbouring Athenaeum. The rear elevation that will be concealed as a result is an example of mural articulation derived from 18th century French architectural theorists. Recently the gallery has housed a café designed by Stephenson Architecture.

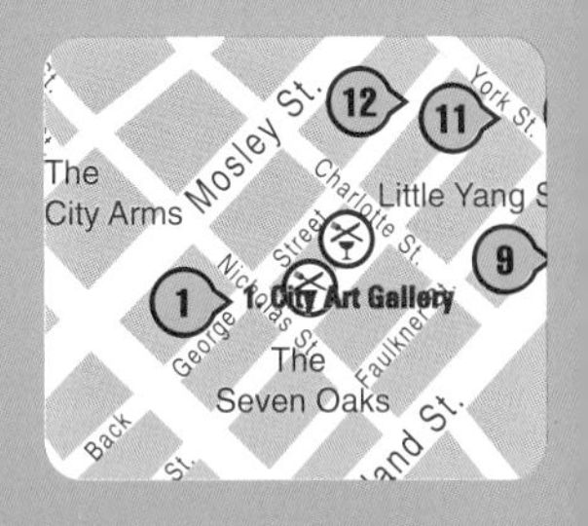

2. National Museum of Labour History/ Mechanics' Institute

Grade II*

103 Princess Street

J.E. Gregan (1854)

A fine Victorian palazzo. The main red brick and buff sandstone elevation to Princess Street has three major storeys and a blind attic storey above cornice level. The use of the palazzo model can be seen in the treatment of the windows. First floor piano nobile windows are highly elaborated with segmental arched pediments. The main entrances are emphasised by arched elaboration and a small projecting first floor level canopy. The composition skilfully maximises the façade to Princess Street and disguises the lozenge-shaped site. Side elevations step back and are more three-dimensionally expressive than the main façade. In stark contrast, the rear of the building is austere in stock and white glazed brick with functionally placed windows and minimal decorative expression. The building is notable for being the site of the first meeting of the Co-operative Insurance Company (now CIS) in 1867 and of the first Trades Union Congress in 1868.

3. Lancaster House Grade II*

67-71 Whitworth Street

Harry S. Fairhurst (1906-12)

Lancaster House is notable for its decoration and compositional inventiveness. Supported by a steel frame, this huge building fully exploits the modelling possibilities offered by brown terracotta and brick. Above a stone basement plinth, the Edwardian Baroque façade successfully hides the bulk of the construction behind. Terracotta is used to provide vertical emphasis to the entrances and stairs and a variety of window shapes and frame details. The corner tower to Princess Street is remarkable, rising through 12 levels of increasing elaboration to a terminating belvedere. Lancaster House shares a common plinth and eaves with its contemporary neighbour, India House (also by Fairhurst and converted into flats), this connection being reinforced by an ornate two storey high circular Art Nouveau wrought iron gate with pendant lamp.

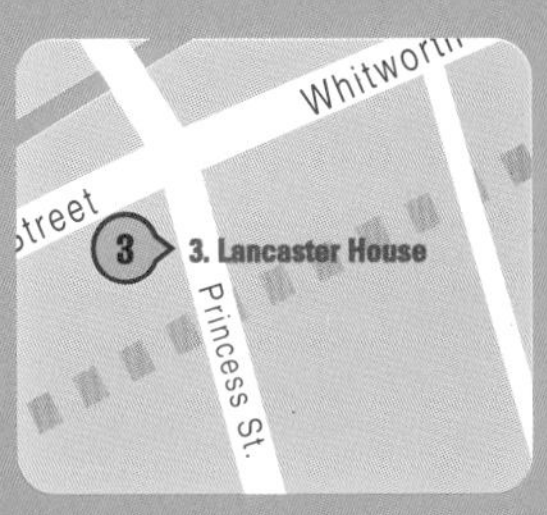

4. Manto

46 Canal Street

Benedict Smith Architects (1989)

The first bar to open up its front onto Canal Street in the late 80s, this conversion of a low industrial space was followed by many imitators as neighbours and beyond. Developing the Dry Bar (see page 109) idiom, the relatively shallow but wide space exploits the shop window potential with vivid colours, exposed steelwork and upper-level balconies. Paired staircases emphasise the symmetry of the bar space which effectively stretches to the canal wall. A recent roof top terrace has introduced a Californian feel using laminated timber beams to suspend the popular first floor balcony.

5. Mash & Air

40 Chorlton Street

Pod (Marc Newson) with Harrison Ince (1996)

Representing a significant style change among Manchester café-bars, Mash & Air looks less to the past for its aesthetic than to a supposedly streamlined, computer generated future. Toned in orange and lime green, predominant circle and port-hole motifs give drinkers and diners on three floors a view on to a technological pleasure totem, a gleaming micro-brewery. The design concept is betrayed however by the poor resolution of some of the detailing, notably the interface between futuristic interior and Victorian warehouse exterior.

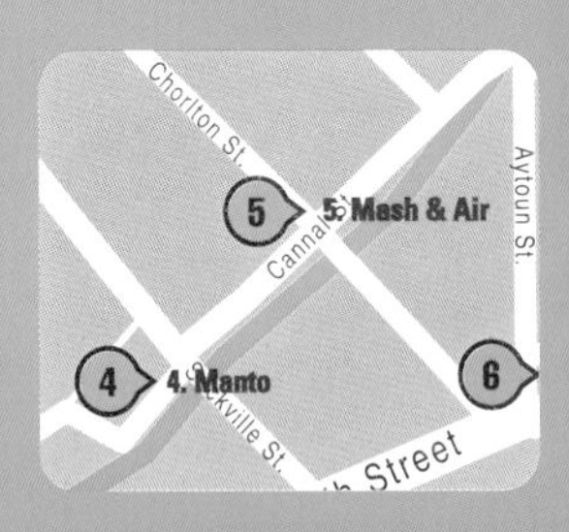

6. Manchester Metropolitan University Aytoun Library

Aytoun Street

Mills Beaumont Leavey Channon (1994)

Erected at great speed, and despite its reliance on the material and formal language of the American architect Richard Meier, the new white building for Manchester Metropolitan University successfully integrates into a largely brick and terracotta context. The elegant curve of the building resolves the awkwardness of the site, while its fluid form echoes that of the nearby Gateway House (see page 113). A double height ramp space internalises an elevation originally destined to be external and is indicative of the generosity with which the building was designed, ostensibly as an addition to an undistinguished existing tower block.

7. London Road Fire Station

Grade II*

London Road

Woodhouse, Willoughby & Langham (1906)

Housing a fire station, police station and coroner's court (still in operation), this buff terracotta and red brick building fills an entire triangular block. The central space can be viewed through the main gates off London Road, revealing an institutional courtyard used for drills overlooked by several storeys of tenement balconies and the fire training tower. The complex functional programme of the building, including gymnasium, library, stables, a bank and flats for over 40 firemen, policemen and families is housed behind Baroque façades common to the period. Encrusted with years of grime, the building presents a romantic silhouette and frequent proposals for conversion to hotel use have failed to materialise. The completeness of the surviving ensemble is due to its occupation until the 1980s.

KICKS

8. S. & J. Watts Warehouse / Britannia Hotel Grade II*

35-47 Portland Street

Traviss & Mangnall (1851)

Manchester's most grandiose textile warehouse innovates the Italian palazzo model through its use of a different architectural style for each floor. Using 27,000 square feet of glass, 40,000 cubic feet of timber, 5,600 tons of sandstone and 700 tons of iron, the massive and ornately decorated structure still dominates Portland Street. Most dramatic are the four pavilions of the top-most floor. Here the combination of the rose windows and the exuberant skyline reflect the commercial optimism that produced the building. Its subsequent conversion to a hotel in the 1980s seems entirely appropriate.

9. Bank of England

Portland Street

Fitzroy Robinson (1971)

Portland Street loses its form and coherence as it approaches Piccadilly and the Bank of England development is one of the culprits. A zone of planting screens the black granite podium of the megastructure. Above and jettying out over the landscape strip is the bank proper and the office tower, Bank Chambers. The former is polished granite and Portland stone, with projecting chamfered bays, and an overhanging cornice-cum-plant space. Bank Chambers is a more conventional tower with bronzed glazing and cream panelling. Neither element, competently handled, adds much to the quality of their urban context.

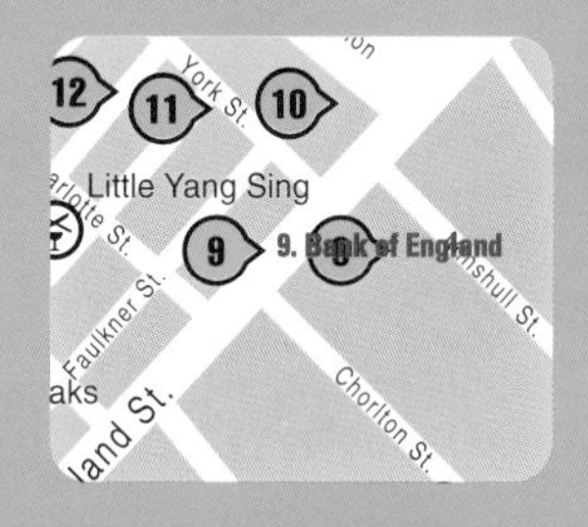

10. Piccadilly Plaza

Piccadilly Gardens

Covell Matthews & Partners (1959-65)

Manchester's architectural equivalent of Concorde (the aeroplane), the scheme exploits images of advanced technology for its decorative motifs, the circuit board-like end elevations of Sunley Tower being an obvious example. It represented a dramatic upwards shift in scale as four of the city's 19th century blocks were combined to create one new super block. A major office tower, a lower hotel slab overhanging Portland Street and a diagonally aligned smaller office tower with a hyperbolic paraboloid roof, sit on a two storey podium. Originally conceived with retail throughout, the podium covers the entire site but has not proved successful. The building's scale and optimism is reflected in the hotel foyer which at the time was the largest concrete cantilevered structure in Europe. The most dynamic element of the scheme is the spiral ramp off York Street which provides access to the hotel and multi-storey car park.

11. Telephone Exchange/ Rutherford House

34 George Street

Ministry of Public Buildings and Works (1967)

Despite its dilapidated condition, this building demonstrates a sophisticated and controlled design aesthetic. Its Italian Rationalist inspired elevation to George Street refers to the work of Guiseppe Terragni. Plane and grid are skilfully manipulated, articulating the fenestration to reflect the activities taking place in the offices within and expressing the framed structure of the building. The base of the building continues the restraint shown in the office slab with a mixture of real and reconstituted stone cladding relieved by large glazed openings to George Street mirrored by service doors to Back George Street.

Planning records for this building do not exist because it is built over an extensive system of nuclear bunkers and the A-bomb proof exchange, Guardian.

12. Portico Library/The Bank

Grade II*

57 Mosley Street

Thomas Harrison (1806)

A local product of the Grand Tour, Harrison designed the home for the Manchester Literary and Philosophical Society in the radical Greek taste. Its temple form comprises an Ionic portico to Mosley Street, and an engaged colonnade to Charlotte Street. Utterly restrained on the exterior, the surviving interior of the library itself is also worthy of note. Although a floor was inserted at the original gallery level during its use as a bank (the former banking hall became a bar in the late 1980s), the glass saucer dome can still be glimpsed from Charlotte Street. The library is referred to by Thomas de Quincy in "Confessions of an Opium-Eater".

Route 5

Recommended Places To Eat & Drink

Victoria Station Bar *Victoria Station*
Jolly Angler *Ducie Street*

1. Nynex Arena/Manchester Evening News Arena

Victoria Street

Austin Smith Lord with Ellerbe Beckett (1995)

This huge scheme can be seen as wasted opportunity. The accommodation includes a multiplex cinema and a multi-purpose arena, plus associated multi-storey parking. Unfortunately these activities are housed in a building which is spatially incomprehensible. Partially sited in air rights space over Victoria Station (see page 103), the scheme originally included proposals for a glass tower which would terminate the views along Deansgate. This has not yet been realised. The architectural design and detailing does not successfully accommodate the large scale of the building or adequately respond to the topographically complex nature of its site. The building's major achievement was its construction over Victoria Station without disrupting its day-to-day use. The weak commercial architectural language is especially evident when approaching from Cheetham Hill to the north.

& YORKSHIRE
VICTORIA

2. Victoria Station Grade II

Victoria Station Approach

Original station and roof:
George Stephenson for the Manchester & Leeds Railway Co. (1844)
Alterations and enlargements:
William Dawes for the Lancashire & Yorkshire Railway Co. (1909)

The long elevation of Victoria Station presents the visitor with Manchester's finest port of entry. Eclectically classical with segmental pediments breaking the skyline, the wrought iron canopy lists some of the exotic destinations available (Scarborough, Fleetwood, Goole...). Internally, the provincial splendour continues with the tiled plan of the Lancashire and Yorkshire Railway, the fine timber ticket office that echoes in miniature the dignity of the station exterior, and the exposed glass dome of the "restaurant". The roof of the train shed itself is a remarkable example of the ingenuity of the 19th century engineers. Downgraded in importance, the station now also serves the Metrolink tram system, and outlying platforms were sacrificed for the construction of the new indoor Manchester Evening News Arena (see page 101).

3. CIS Tower *Grade II*

Miller Street

G.S. Hay and Sir John Burnet Tait & Partners, with interiors by Sir Misha Black / The Design Research Unit (1962)

In the canon of post-WW2 Modernist buildings in Manchester, this is undoubtedly the best. The building refers to the mature work of the American architects Skidmore Owens & Merrill. Two asymmetrically balanced towers rise from a plaza with a lower horizontal block. The predominant materials are steel and glass, counterpointed by the higher service tower in solid unadorned mosaic. A mural by George Mitchell adorns the imposing entrance lobby. The thoroughness with which this important provincial institution, the Cooperative Insurance Society, adopted this transatlantic style suggests that it was seeking to shed its cloth cap roots and embrace a more contemporary corporate image.

4. Daily Express Grade II*

Great Ancoats Street

Sir Owen Williams (1939)

Without the Art Deco motifs of its sister building in London's Fleet Street, this building has been described by Sir Nikolaus Pevsner as "the best building in Manchester between the wars". Employing Williams's characteristic black vitrolite cladding and horizontal ribbon windows, the building consists of offices over a double height press hall exposed to Great Ancoats Street. The building is not only functionally explicit, it is also functionally styled, as witnessed by the streamlined corners, the towers, the expressed cladding joints and the continuous window cleaning carrier rail which the architectural critic Kenneth Frampton has described as virtually Williams's signature. Recently, the building has been converted into offices with the introduction of a mezzanine to the Press Hall, which diminishes the presence of this space on the street.

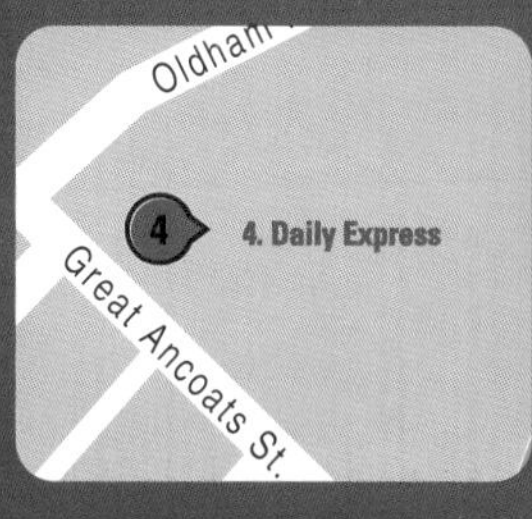

5. Urban Splash/ Smithfield Buildings

Oldham Street/Tib Street

Stephenson Bell (1998)

Occupying an entire block in the Northern Quarter, this loft development integrates a series of commercial and warehouse buildings into a showpiece for the area. The exterior reveals the history of the block; the refurbished upper storeys are largely original, while the lower and ground storeys are treated in a uniform post-industrial manner to accommodate a layer of shops. The building reaches out to its less salubrious surroundings by means of a graphically exuberant stained glass bridge crossing Tib Street to the adjacent Church Street car park which has a stair tower converted to Manchester's very own, if minuscule, Empire State Building (radio mast). The building has been awarded a 1998 RIBA Award for Architecture as an example of the best new British architecture.

6. Dry 201

28 Oldham Street

Ben Kelly Design (1989)

Dry represents the prototypical 'Manchester bar'. Built to provide a meeting place for Hacienda-bound clubbers, the scheme reused an existing retail space to create an extensive bar and restaurant. Employing a palette developed from Ben Kelly's earlier Hacienda (see page 135), the design uses bold colours, witty retention of found details (the curtain preserved in plaster in the front area), locally referenced details (the spear penetrating the Spear Street façade), specially designed furniture by Jasper Morrison and untreated industrial materials to produce a striking contemporary space which has undoubtedly influenced the majority of subsequent Manchester bars.

BRASSERIE

7. Joshua Hoyle & Co./ Malmaison Hotel Grade II

London Road

J.W. Beaumont (1905)

Darby Associates (1998)

This fine Edwardian façade was narrowly saved from demolition in the late 1980s and in its new guise as part of the Malmaison Hotel continues to greet visitors as they arrive at Piccadilly Station. The green terracotta base supports six storeys of turn-of-the-century swagger. Cream terracotta bays pierce a layered brick surface, combining with an elaborate roofline of gables and a turret on the angled corner. The new extension is far from timid, with its own glazed tower and canopied entrance, while the rear elevation tries to imitate the exuberance of the highly original colour scheme by means of a flat panelled surface. A particularly noteworthy feature of the original building (and entirely typical of its date) is the fenestration treatment of the staircase, with staggered windows and diaper patterns in a shallow arched vertical frame.

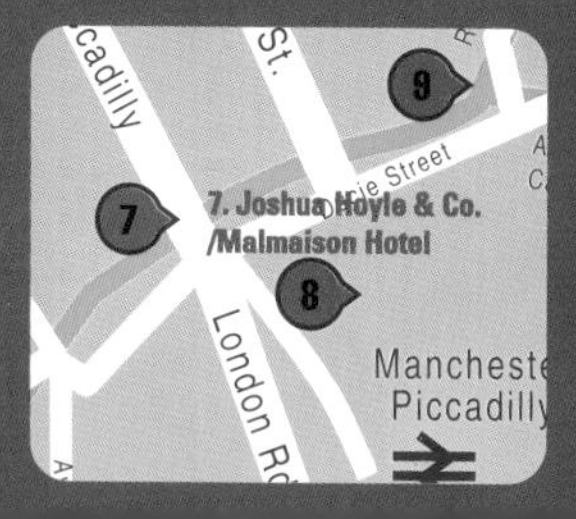

8. Gateway House

Piccadilly Station Approach

R. Seifert & Partners (1969)

Producing a lazy 'S' sweep up to Piccadilly Station, this building provides retail accommodation at ground level and also first floor level towards Ducie Street, with offices above. The horizontality of the scheme is emphasised through the treatment of the façades, which make extensive use of anodised aluminium and minimally detailed strip-glazing. The scheme provides a striking Modern image appropriate to the move from steam trains to diesel and electric. Unfortunately, Piccadilly Station concourse provides a disappointing architectural and spatial conclusion to the route up Station Approach.

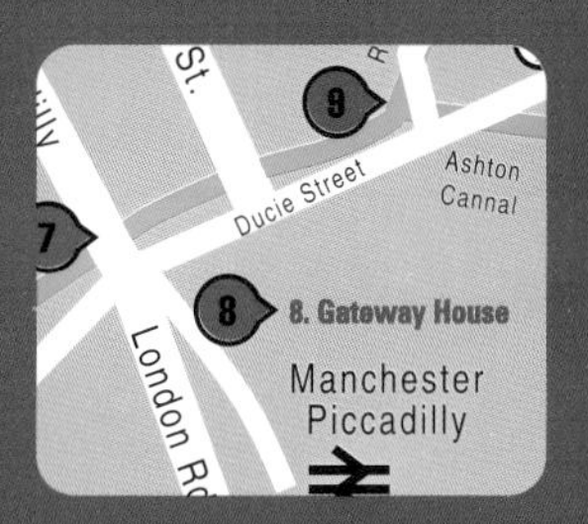

9. Rochdale Canal

(some parts Grade II)

Rochdale Canal Company (1804-1805)

The first major transport infrastructure running through central Manchester, the Rochdale Canal was constructed to feed the city's booming trade and industry during the Industrial Revolution, linking with the Bridgewater Canal in Castlefield. The canal is an excellent example of industrial architecture of the era, with fine functionally detailed sandstone and brickwork along its length. The restored locks exemplify well-considered use of these materials in conjunction with timber lock gates and cast iron fixtures. The striking difference between the functionally designed canal and towpath, and the picturesque domestic accommodation of the lock keeper's cottages is particularly evident at the Dukes 92 lock in Castlefield. The canal now provides a spatially dramatic east-west armature for pedestrians and joggers, and connects many of the buildings mentioned in this guide. Please note that the length of the canal crosses many of the routes in this guide. A walk down the canal itself provides an interesting cross-section of the architecture of Manchester.

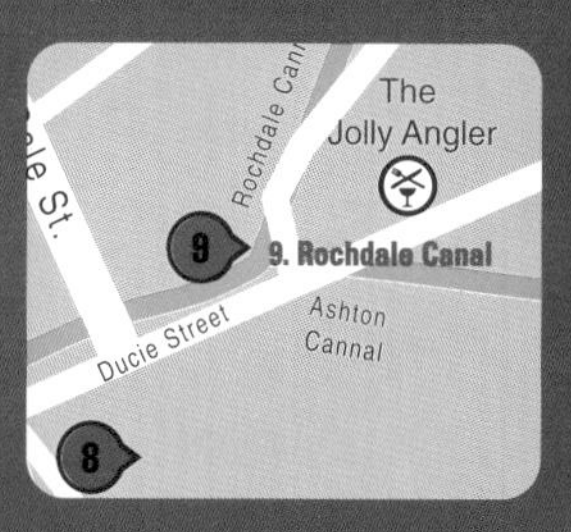

Route 6

Recommended Places
To Eat & Drink

Java Bar Expresso *Oxford Road Station Approach*
The Crown *Deansgate*

1. Oxford Road Train Station

Grade II

Oxford Road Station Approach

W.R. Headley, succeeded by R.L. Moorcroft (1960)

Its skyline marks this out as one of the most dramatic train stations in England. The dynamic laminated timber conoid shell roof was developed by engineer Max Glendinning as a response to a difficult triangular site and was originally to be realised in concrete. Currently undergoing major refurbishment, the original building is characterised by bold and consistent timber detailing. This can be seen in the platform canopy edges and the ticket offices and station café, which are treated as elements beneath the main roof. Subsequent prefabricated additions such as the waiting rooms and the new tubular steel structure compromise the high architectural standard of the original vision.

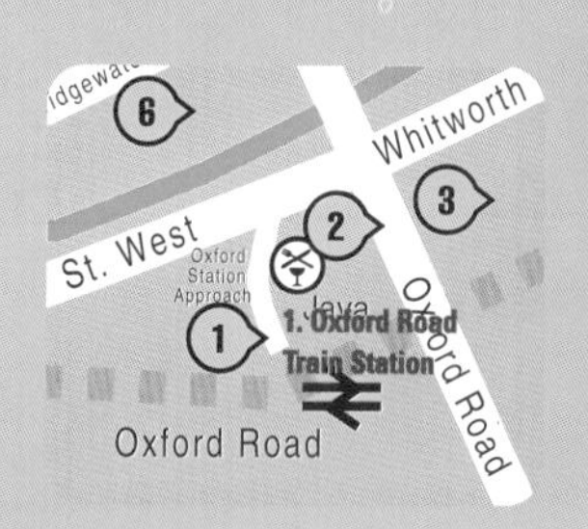

CORNERHOUSE CINEMAS
LOVE IS
THE DEVIL 18
MEN WITH
GUNS 15

2. Cornerhouse Arts Centre

70 Oxford Street

The Millard Partnership and Fletcher Priest Architects (1985) Refurbishment: David Chipperfield (1998)

The Cornerhouse, with its galleries and cinema, is located in two buildings facing each other over Oxford Road Station Approach. Together they are an early example of the creative reuse of existing buildings for the arts in Manchester, in this case a former department store and cinema. The main building is an Edwardian flat iron building into which a ground floor bar, two basement cinemas, upper levels of galleries and a first floor restaurant were inserted in a non-descript style. Externally, a rather bulky white pressed metal signage band and new windows were added.

The cinema opposite has been refitted since the original refurbishment. David Chipperfield Architects have introduced a dramatic façade of glass planks with a bright double-height yellow and white foyer space behind. The scheme now acts as a beacon on the junction of Whitworth Street and Oxford Road, defines the cinema entrance and adds an appropriately modern image to Manchester's most innovative independent cinema.

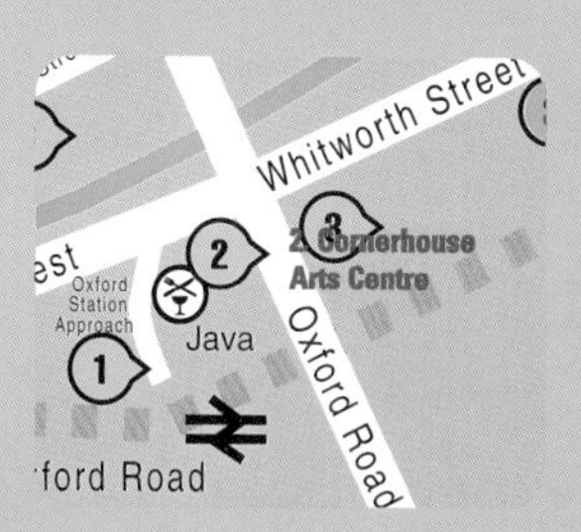

3. Refuge Assurance/Palace Hotel Grade II*

Oxford Street

Alfred Waterhouse (1891)

Paul Waterhouse (1910 & 1913)

The cutting of Whitworth Street in the 1890s resulted in a series of large self-confident buildings along it. A monument to insurance, the mammoth Refuge building exploits the full possibilities of architectural ceramics. Its interior employs white glazed brick for the former office space, but the exterior exploits the potential of terracotta for insistent repetitive ornament over large surfaces. Articulated frames to the high windows culminate in barley-sugar columns, while the great brick tower is a landmark in many directions. The porte cochere beneath it, with its glazed dome and memorial to the company's war dead, is now the reception for the Palace Hotel which currently occupies this dramatic and robust building.

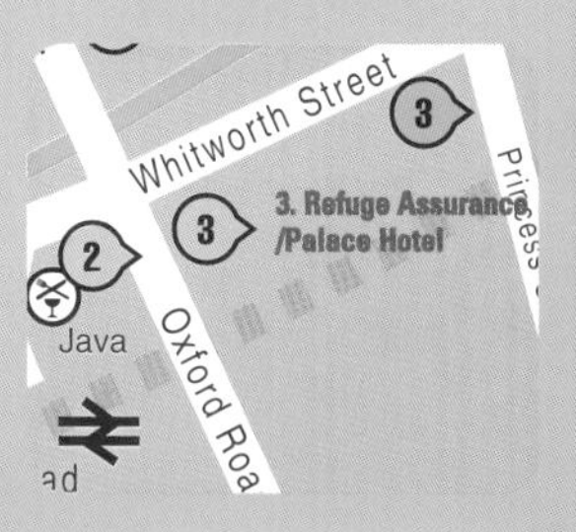

4. St. James' Buildings Grade II

65-95 Oxford Street

Clegg, Fryer & Penman (1912)

Exuberant Edwardian Baroque struggles to reduce the massive scale of the long Portland stone elevation of this building. The façade fronted over 1000 rooms and contributes to the diverse range of architectural styles in evidence on this stretch of Oxford Street. The lower three storeys are rusticated to form a base with heavily modelled windows, the ends and centre of the elevation expressed as pavilions. Above four storeys of framed windows sit on a planar ground on top of which is a storey of triple windows punched into the façade below the cornice. An elaborate central tower marks the main entrance. Recently, the lower storey has been refurbished to give continuity to the signage of the shops, marred by the introduction of a remarkably crude neo-Art Nouveau canopy over the building's main entrance.

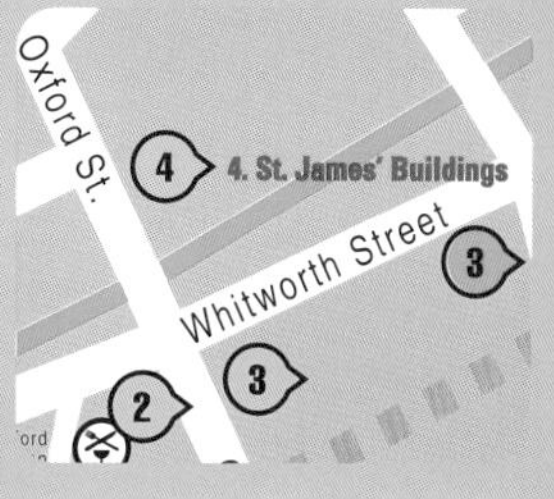

5. Canada House Grade II

3 Chepstow Street

William G. Higginbottom (1909)

A good example of mainstream Edwardian warehouse/office design. The framed construction is revealed by the extensive glazed elevations, with the more public façades being clad in elaborate buff terracotta employing a wide range of eclectic, classically inspired motifs with Art Nouveau iron work. The five major storeys meet the street line, with two attic storeys set back and revealing a more functional form. A comparison of the façade now facing towards Oxford Road with the three major façades reveals the different architectural approach to public and non-public faces of the building. Terracotta is dispensed with to reveal a cast-iron frame of semi-recessed octagonal columns, defining three window wide, five storey high bays of unembellished sash windows. This façade's functional language relates to the attic storeys and is surprisingly modern in feel.

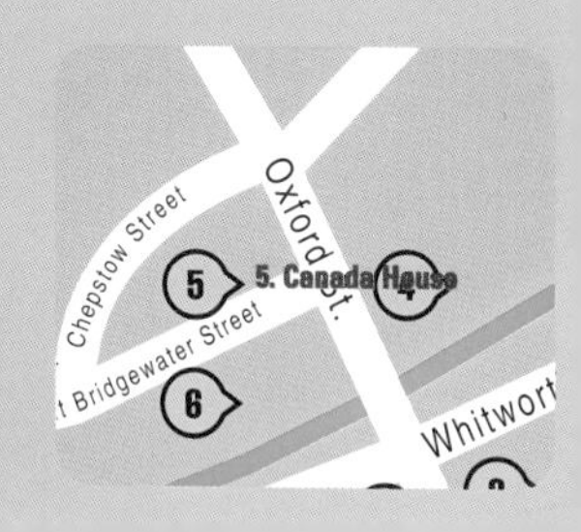

6. Lee House Grade II

90 Great Bridgewater Street

Harry S. Fairhurst & Son (1931)

Quintessentially Art Deco in style, Lee House is the base of an unrealised 17 storey vertical warehouse. Now in use as offices, the elevations show the influence of American skyscraper design of the period. Strong masonry corners frame extensively glazed, vertically accentuated, shallow bays. The windows and spandrel panels, originally framed in bronze, provide a subtle modelling to the surface of an essentially rather bulky building. The cornice is replaced with a window cleaning cradle rail supported on stylised brackets and aligns in height with the adjacent Tootal Building of 33 years earlier.

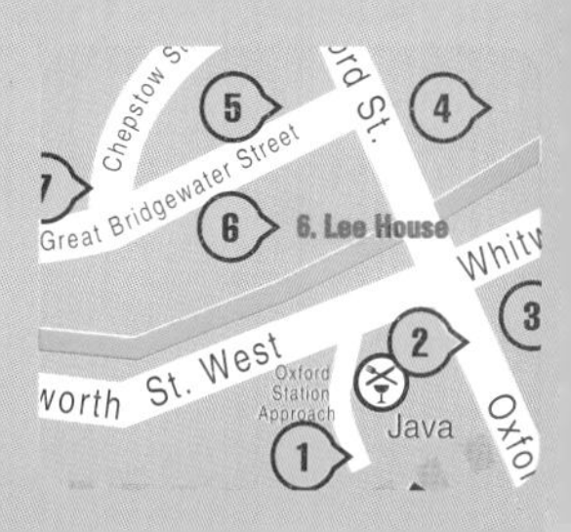

OF
BEER, WINES &
ON or OFF THE PREMISES

7. Peveril of the Peak Grade II

127 Chepstow Street

Original architects unknown (c. 1820 altered c. 1900)

On a narrow triangular plot formed by converging strips of canal edge industrial development, the low scale of the building indicates its early date. Most of what is visible dates from the refurbishment at the turn of the century. Externally covered in green glazed tiles with jolly if rudimentary classical detail, the interior furnishings are remarkable now as authentic survivals in the era of theme pubs. Despite the clearance of large parts of the original surrounding context, the building retains a distinctive public presence beyond its small size. A particular highlight is the table football machine.

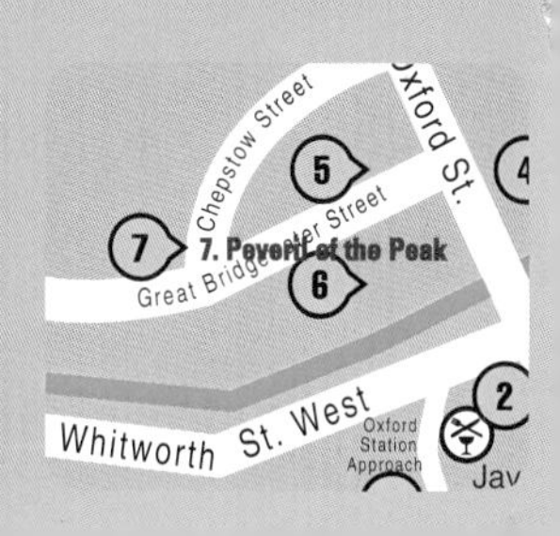

8. Bridgewater Hall

Lower Mosley Street

Renton Howard Wood Levin (1996)

Home to the Hallé Orchestra and acoustically superior to the now disused Free Trade Hall (see page 67), the Bridgewater Hall fails to create a meaningful link with Albert Square and the Town Hall (see page 55), which was the reason for its alignment. The exterior is clothed in a language derived from contemporary commercial and leisure buildings, attempting to create a visual interest while failing to express the formally simple idea of the building as an 'egg in a box'. The concert hall is surrounded by a series of foyers echoing the architect Hans Scharoun's 1960s Philharmonie in Berlin. The building is notable for its new canal basin off the Rochdale Canal (see page 115) which offers the opportunity to arrive for a concert by barge, and is the centrepiece of the adjacent linked commercial development.

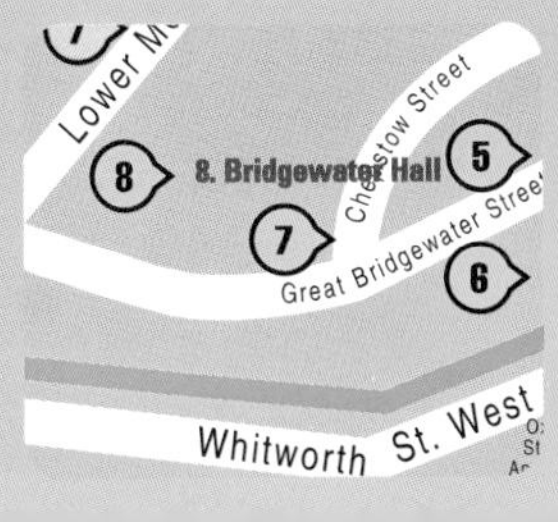

9. The Hacienda:Fac 51

13, Whitworth Street West

Ben Kelly Design (1982)

Shortly to be demolished to make way for a new development, this night club is famous for its influence on design and dance music. In a former yacht factory, it employed a language of bold graphics and colours to create a post-industrial social space which became the accepted architectural language for Manchester bars. Initially poor acoustically, the interior used industrial materials, including traffic bollards and yellow and black warning markings to define the dancefloor in conjunction with a number of post-modern decorative motifs such as a faux-ruined archway. The latter compromised the industrial chic of the club and its record label Factory Records. Ben Kelly later designed the Dry 201 bar on Oldham Street (see page 109).

10. British Council Headquarters/British Telecommunications

Grand Island Site, Medlock Street

Building Design Partnership (1991)

Located on the site of the former Gaythorn gasworks, this scheme was constructed in response to the relocation of the British Council from London. Set amid extensive uninspired landscaping, the building meets the functional needs of the brief through a simple, grey-clad, square doughnut in plan, with offices overlooking a central atrium. This features artworks and installations by major contemporary British artists such as Patrick Heron. The surrounding landscaping coupled with the building's location relative to Whitworth Street railway viaduct isolates the building as an object from the dense urban pattern to the north.

11. Planet 4 Studios

2-4 Little Peter Street

Simpson Associates (1995)

This recording studio reuses and adds to a small existing early 19th century building. It is an example of the creative industries that have been recolonising the formerly derelict Knott Mill area. The entrance is treated in a simple planar manner, the most dramatic feature being the glass block shower pod which tops the scheme. This project is a good example of how contemporary architects are sympathetically reusing old buildings to create schemes which are fresh and modern.

12. Atlas

376 Deansgate

Simpson Associates (1994)

Reusing the name and the premises of a defunct motor repair workshop, Atlas effectively exploits its location and internal space to produce a bar with three characters. The front space aligns itself with Deansgate. The fully glazed elevations provide a successful link with the street and an exciting location to watch the traffic swerve to avoid the building. The central space, in a railway arch underneath Deansgate Station, is relatively introspective. This contrasts with the open rear external terrace (designed by Landscape Projects) with its extensive views to the River Medlock and the Bridgewater Canal spur. The scheme is given coherence by the use of self-finished plywood internal cladding and reclaimed floorboards throughout, which continues as timber decking on the terrace.

13. Castlefield Viaduct

Castlefield

The Midland Railway Co. (c. 1880)

Historically, Castlefield functioned as a city edge where goods were delivered to the industrial centre. The impact of this can now be observed in the multiple layering of transport infrastructures. Castlefield Viaduct bridges over the earlier Rochdale Canal. The cast iron viaduct is an excellent example of the 19th century attitude to engineering. Its heroic brute scale is romanticised by the castellated turrets adorning the structure. The building of this and similarly large nearby structures has given the city some of its most dramatic spaces, Piranesian in their quality. Partly in use for Metrolink services, the viaduct provides a dynamic viewpoint for the whole of Castlefield. Through the reconfiguration and reuse of this previously defunct infrastructure, this area was the most visible expression of the existence of the Central Manchester Development Corporation between 1987 and 1997, although its gentrification has produced a lessening of the dramatic impact of the original host structures.

14. Barça

Catalan Square

Harrison Ince (1996)

The dernier cri of 1996, Barça on Catalan Square epitomises Manchester's European aspirations in a cacophony of Deconstructivist motifs. These include the re-use of a railway viaduct, collisions of banal post-industrial details, faux-ruined rear elevation, and an apparently random selection of designer furniture. Angled brickwork and glass block, five bar checker plate, crudely welded steel details, heavy chains, and the inevitable burnt orange and ultramarine colour scheme produce the apotheosis of the 'Manchester Bar'.

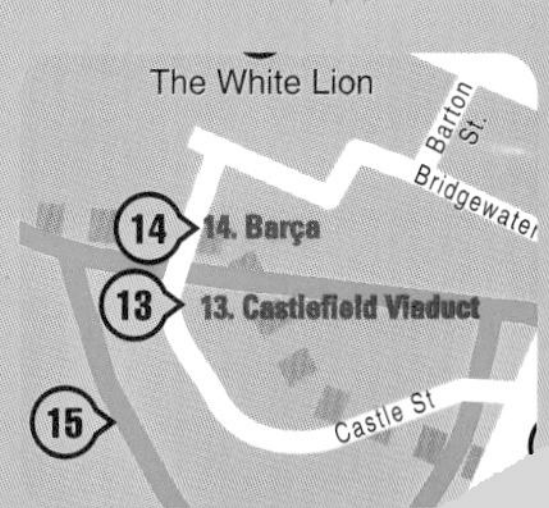

15. Merchants Bridge

Catalan Square

Whitby & Bird (1996)

This dramatic curved bridge spans the Castlefield basin and lies on the route between Barça and Quay Bar. The design relied heavily on computer analysis for its final resolution and introduces a sweeping dynamic curve across the canal: its structural adventurousness can be felt as you walk over it. Its use of white painted steel contrasts a strong contemporary image with the surrounding 18th and 19th century urban fabric. It is one of a number of striking new bridges which have been used in Manchester to provide strong visual foci and to promote development.

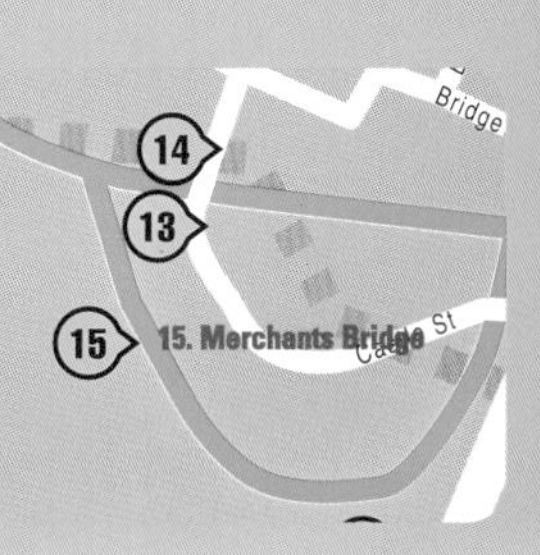

16. Quay Bar

Bridgewater Viaduct, Deansgate

Stephenson Bell (1998)

This project received a Royal Academy Summer Exhibition prize when it was presented in model form. With its planning based on spiral geometry inspired by the site, the building sits adjacent to Bridgewater Viaduct looking over Castlefield canal basin. At street level its presence is announced by a light tower. From the street the bar is reached by a ramped bridge which enters at the upper level of a double height space. Full height glazing, supported by airfoil section structural fins addresses the canal. The intention to create a series of layered spaces opening out towards the canal is not completely successful and the detailing is sometimes unresolved, but the terrace to the canal works well. On completion the building was awarded a 1998 RIBA Award for Architecture as an example of the best new British architecture.

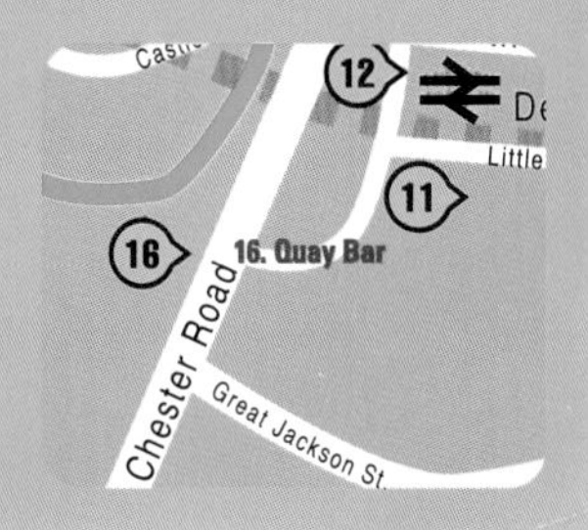

Index of Architects

Austin Smith Lord Nynex Arena/ Manchester Evening News Arena (1995) 101
Austin Sztrala Turner Y.M.C.A./St. George's House (1992) 71
Barry, Sir Charles City Art Gallery (1835) 77
Beaumont, J.S. Kendal's (1939) 25
Beaumont, J.W. Joshua Hoyle & Co./Malmaison Hotel (1905) 111
Benedict Smith Architects (1989) Manto 83
Black, Sir Misha CIS Tower (1962) 105
Bradshaw, Gass & Hope Royal Exchange (1921) 19
Building Design Partnership British Council HQ/ BritishTelecom(1991) 135
Burnet, Sir John, Tait & Partners CIS Tower (1962) 105
Calatrava, Santiago Trinity Bridge (1996) 27
Casson Conder & Partners Former National Westminster Bank Northern Headquarters (1969) 37
Champneys, Basil Manchester Cathedral (1898 and 1903) 9
Rylands Library (1899) 33
Chipperfield, David Cornerhouse Arts Centre (1998) 121
Clegg, Fryer & Penman St. James' Buildings (1912) 125
Cockerell, Charles Robert Former Bank of England (1846) 35
Corbett, Raby & Sawyer Barton Arcade (1871) 23
Covell Matthews & Partners Piccadilly Plaza (1965) 93
Crowther, J.S. Manchester Cathedral (1886) 9
Darby Associates Joshua Hoyle & Co./Malmaison Hotel (1998) 111
Dawes, William Victoria Station (1909) 103
Design Research Unit CIS Tower (1962) 105
Ellerbe Beckett Nynex Arena/Manchester Evening News Arena (1995) 101
Essex Goodman & Suggit Central Station/GMEX (1985) 69
Fairhurst, Harry S. Lancaster House (1912)
Lee House (1931) 81
Fitzroy Robinson Bank of England (1971) 91
Fletcher Priest Architects Cornerhouse Arts Centre (1985) 121
Fowler, Sir John Central Station/GMEX (1879) 69
Great Northern Railway Co. Great Northern Railway Company's Goods Warehouse (1896) 65
Gregan, J.E. National Museum of Labour History/Mechanics' Institute (1854) 79
Harris, E. Vincent Central Reference Library (1934) 45
Town Hall Extension (1938) 47
Harrison Ince Barça (1996) 139
Mash & Air (1996) 83
Harrison, Thomas Portico Library/The Bank (1806) 97
Hartas, Thomas Manchester Law Library (1885) 41
Hay, G.S. CIS Tower (1962) 105
Headley, W.R. Oxford Road Train Station (1960) 119
Heywood, Oliver & Charles Chetham's School (1885) 11
Higginbottom, William G. Canada House (1909) 127
Holden, J.P. Manchester Cathedral (1815 & 1868) 9
Holford Associates Former Bank of England (1995) 35
Howitt, L.C. (Manchester City Architect) Free Trade Hall (1952) 67
Crown Square Crown Court (1962) 31
Kelly Design, Ben The Hacienda:Fac 51 (1982) 135
Dry 201 (1989) 109

Lancashire & Yorkshire Railway Co.
Victoria Station (1909) 103
Lane, Richard
Friends' Meeting House (1828) 49
Leach, Rhodes & Walker
Crown Square Scottish Life House (now Manchester House) (1965) 31
Crown Square Cumberland House (1967) 31
Levitt Bernstein
Royal Exchange Theatre, (1976; 1998) 19
Liverpool & Manchester Railway Co.
Liverpool Road Station and Museum of Science & Industry (1830) 59
Lutyens, Sir Edwin
Midland Bank (1929) 39
Cenotaph (1924) 43
Manchester & Leeds Railway Co.
Victoria Station (1844) 103
Midland Railway Co.
Central Station/ GMEX (1879) 69
Castlefield Viaduct (c. 1880) 139
The Millard Partnership
Cornerhouse Arts Centre (1985) 121
Mills Beaumont Leavey Channon
Manchester Metropolitan University Aytoun Library (1994) 85
Ministry of Public Buildings & Works
Telephone Exchange/Rutherford House (1967) 95
Moorcroft, R.L.
Oxford Road Train Station (1960) 119
Pod (Marc Newson) Mash & Air (1996) 83
Potts, Son & Pickup
Corn Exchange (1903) 13
Renton Howard Wood Levin
Bridgewater Hall (1996) 133
Richardson & Gill, with Farquarson
Opera House (1912) 63
Rochdale Canal Company
Rochdale Canal (1805) 115
Seifert, R. & Partners
Gateway House (1969) 113
Simpson Associates Atlas (1994) 137
Planet 4 Studios (1995) 137
Stephenson Bell Urban
Splash/Smithfield Buildings (1998) 109
Quay Bar (1998) 143
Stephenson, George
Liverpool Road Station and Museum of Science & Industry (1830) 59
Victoria Station (1844) 103
Sunlight, Joseph Sunlight House (1932) 65
Traviss & Mangnall S. & J. Watts Warehouse/Britannia Hotel (1851) 89
Trubshaw, Charles Midland Hotel (1903) 73
Tubbs, Ralph Granada Television (1962) 61
Walters, Edward Free Trade Hall (1856) 67
Waterhouse, Alfred
Manchester Town Hall (1877) 55
Chetham's School (1878) 11
St. Ann's Church (1891) 21
Refuge Assurance/Palace Hotel (1891) 123
Waterhouse, Paul Refuge Assurance/Palace Hotel (1913) 123
Whinney, Son & Ansten Hall
Midland Bank (1929) 39
Whitby & Bird Merchants Bridge (1996) 141
Williams, Sir Owen Daily Express (1939) 107
Wilson & Wormersley
Arndale Centre (1979) 17
Woodhouse, Corbett & Dean
Y.M.C.A./St. George's House (1909) 71
Woodhouse, Willoughby & Langham
London Road Fire Station (1906) 87
Worthington, Sir Hubert Manchester Cathedral (post-1940) 9
Worthington, Sir Percy
Manchester Cathedral (1934) 9
Worthington, Thomas
Albert Memorial (1862) 53
Memorial Hall Square Albert (1865) 51
Wren, Sir Christopher
St. Ann's Church (1712) 21
Yorke, Rosenberg & Mardall
Crown Square Magistrates' Court (1971) 31

Glossary

Art Deco: A style of design associated with the 1925 Exposition des Arts Decoratifs in Paris. Its main features were a bold geometry and motifs derived from non-western architectural traditions such as the Egyptian, Assyrian and Pre-Columbian.

Art Nouveau: A style of design associated with the years around the turn of 19th and 20th centuries. Its principal features were the use of organic motifs and the innovative use of new materials.

Ashlar: Smooth dressed horizontally coursed stone masonry.

Baroque: A European style of architecture which originated in 17th century Italy. Free use of classical ornament and contrasting concave and convex forms characterise the style, which was revived in Britain in the Edwardian period.

City of Manchester Plan: Produced under the direction of R. Nicholls in 1945, the Plan was a comprehensive attempt to integrate the reconstruction of war-damaged areas and longer-term planning needs such as the development of motorised transport.

Deconstructivism: A style of architecture from the 1980s based on the application of post structuralist French Literary theory to architecture. Its principal theorist is the American architect Peter Eisenman.

Doric: A Greek order of architecture dating from 600 BC where motifs are a translation into stone of earlier timber construction. The Parthenon in Athens is an example of a Doric Temple.

Edwardian: Referring to the reign of King Edward VII (1901 - 1910), the term can generally be stretched to cover the 1890s up until the outbreak of World War 1 in 1914.

Factory Records: An independent record label founded by Granada TV presenter Tony Wilson in the aftermath of punk. The success of bands such as Joy Division and New Order led to the founding of the nightclub The Hacienda.

Georgian: A style of architecture associated with the reigns of King George I (1714 - 27) George II (1727 - 1760) George III (1760 - 1820) George IV (1820 - 1830). Its predominant features are the use of restrained classical ornament and proportions.

Gothic: A style of architecture derived from the ecclesiastical architecture of Medieval Europe. Featuring organic ornament, it can be identified by its use of the pointed arch. The style was revived in the 19th century, in particular as the result of the writings of Augustus W.N. Pugin in the 1840s.

Hi Tech: A style of architecture associated with the 1970s. Its dramatic celebration of building technology, in particular the expression of servicing elements was derived from the work of the Archigram Group in the 1960s. In Britain its principal exponents are Norman Foster, Richard Rogers, Nicholas Grimshaw.

International Style: A term coined by Philip Johnson and Henry Russell-Hitchcock for an exhibition at the MOMA in New York. It defined modern architecture's characteristics as absence of ornament, purity of form and the use of the flat roof.

Ionic: A Greek order of architecture particularly associated with Greek territories in Asia Minor. The column, sometimes fluted, can be identified by its capital with pairs of scrolled volutes.

Mansard: A type of roof in which a steep pitch is used in the lower portion to provide an area of dormer windows. Derived from the name of the French architect Francois Mansart.

Miséricord: A type of ledge used in Medieval choir stalls to provide relief for the priests during lengthy services. They often feature examples of subversive carving.

Modern: Referring to the 20th century movement which rejected figurative and historical references in architecture. Characterised by simplicity of line, innovative use of materials, industrialised techniques, and new structural forms.

Neo-Classical: A reaction to Baroque or Rococo decorative excesses, archaeologically correct Classical forms are employed within a rational architectural system using pure geometry and resulting in solid and restrained buildings with little or no decoration.

New Cathedral Street: The principal urban design feature of the redevelopment of Manchester City Centre following the IRA bomb of 15 June 1996. It will connect St Ann's Church and the Royal Exchange with the Cathedral and the Corn Exchange.

Northern Quarter: An area of decayed industrial and commercial buildings designated for regeneration by Manchester City Council in 1994, to encourage commercial and residential development.

Palazzo: The Italian word to designate an urban residential building generally arranged around a courtyard. The façade and overhanging cornice were elements copied in the Manchester 'palazzo' warehouse.

Peterloo Massacre: On 16th August 1819 on St. Peter's Field the radical Henry Hunt addressed a crowd of over 30000 on electoral reform. The Manchester Yeomanry attempted to arrest Hunt on the hustings, leaving at least 11 members of the crowd dead and 600 injured. The Free Trade Hall stands on the site of this event.

Pevsner, Sir Nikolaus: A 20th century architectural historian, born in Germany. He is particularly associated with the recording of the Buildings of England by county.

Piano Nobile: An Italian term designating the first floor of a domestic building (generally above workshops or arcades on the ground floor). Characterised by larger windows and richer ornament.

Piranesian: Pertaining to the work of Giovanni Battista Piranesi, an 18th century Italian engraver, archaeologist and architect. Etchings of vast and ruinous spaces are his most characteristic output.

Post-Industrial: Relating to the aesthetic use of industrial building technology and iconography, and the reuse of former industrial buildings.

Post Modern: Relating to architecture which abandoned the doctrines of the Modern movement. Often associated with the revival of enfeebled classical forms in 1980s, its first clear theoretical text was Robert Venturi's *Complexity and Contradiction in Architecture* of 1966.

Rationalism: A form of Modern Movement architecture associated with Italian exponents, most notably the Gruppo Sette including Giuseppe Terragni whose major work is the Casa del Fascio in Como of 1936.

Renaissance: Relating to the 'rebirth' of the architecture and the culture of classical antiquity in Italy during the 15th and 16th centuries.

Ruskin, John: The eminent 19th century art critic notable for his championing of the works of J.M.W Turner and the Pre-Raphaelites. His most influential architectural works were *The Seven Lamps of Architecture* and *The Stones of Venice.*

Serlian: Pertaining to Sebastiano Serlio and his *Five Books of Architecture.* Most usually relating to a 'Serlian' window (also 'Palladian' window) where a central arched window is flanked by two lower rectangular openings. This motif was, in turn, derived from the form of a Roman triumphal arch.

Spandrel: A panel spanning between two vertical elements, or across an arched opening in a wall

Victorian: Relating to the 19th century, but specifically to the reign of Queen Victoria (1837 - 1901).

Vitrolite: An opaque coloured glass sheet material introduced in the 1930s.

Voussoirs: A fan shaped stone or brick, part of a number spanning an opening and typically forming an arch or flat opening.

Ziggurat: A name denoting a stepped pyramid as seen in the temple structures of Ancient Near Eastern and Pre-Columbian American civilisations.